YOGA IN THE MORNING, MARTINI AT NIGHT

or

The First Three-Score and Ten are the Hardest

YOGA IN THE MORNING, MARTINI AT NIGHT

or

The First Three-Score and Ten are the Hardest

Carol Lehman Winfield

Copyright © 2001 by Carol Lehman Winfield

ISBN: 1-58820-345-X

This book is printed on acid free paper.

1stBooks - rev. 1/18/01

DEDICATION

This book is respectfully dedicated to those over seventy
wherever
and whoever you may be.
I honor your struggle and encourage your aspirations,
asking only that you never forget:
OLD IS (HENCE **YOU** ARE) MAGNIFICENT!

ACKNOWLEDGMENTS

Never again will I heedlessly brush past the Acknowledgments page of a book. Having finally completed mine, I now realize its primacy. Without the guidance and buttressing of those listed below, my work could never have achieved so satisfactory a conclusion. Read on, then, and with me recognize the depth and sincerity of my gratitude.

In 1997 when I began, Burton Strom came immediately to my aid. Peerless satirist and wit though he be, never once did that beloved friend direct barbs my way as he patiently encouraged me forward. Following on his heels, photographic artist and irrepressible chum, Rosel Froelich Stone (responsible for the front and back covers) stood staunchly through my meteoric stages of despair.

As for John Kern (and the uncomplaining evenings he spent eating my slapped together dinners), dare I count the hours he worked or place value on his precise, civilized improvements which made it possible for the book to take form? In like manner, brother Eugene H. Lehman, Jr., read and reread--and yet even reread again with unabated approval and applause–all the while issuing meticulous directives, grammatical and linguistic.

Pure serendipity introduced me to Linda Severance Smith at the 1998 League of Vermont Writers' Annual Meeting. One year later, I called for editing help. What began as a professional relationship has metamorphosed, through the book and her participation in my yoga class, into lasting friendship. As an editor, Linda assumes her author's coloration. I am beholden, good friend.

As well, I am beholden to Margaret Johnson, Lea Wood, Maria Tedford, and Georgina La Valley, members of our writing group, for their detailed attention to my work. I still reel from their honest competence.

While on my Kudo Kick, let me pay tribute to my favorite yoga students: The Minimums (3-8 year olds) and The Maximums (over sixty), and to Kathy and Liza of Yoga Vermont,who deftly manage an exceptional yoga center.

I respectfully ask you to indulge an OLD Grandma's attachment to the uncensored contributions of: (1) Prologue and Epilogue writers Rachel Winfield and Eve Crevoshay, respectively; (2) illustrator Zachary Winfield; (3) composer Gideon Crevoshay. Please continue the indulgence by granting me leave to express deep appreciation to Madeleine Winfield Crevoshay, Gregory Alan Winfield, and their spouses, Stephen and Deborah, whose unwavering support sustain me still.

Stand by as I run through other indelibly engraved names. Newport, Vermont: Judy Gibbs, Gloria Thomson, Iola Kelley, and cherished Elaine Rowe. A nod of nostalgia for Betsy of Sweet Adeline, Sandy of Alexandra, and Karen & Christie of Bogner's. New York City: Robert and Rae

Gilsen, Sue Drury, and Lois Sook. Burlington: Let's hear it for my peers at The Body Shop under the tutelage of Yves and Judy Bradley; for Irene Callisto, of Isadora's and Shad at Hard Copy on Main Street.

As for keeping my phsyche in cync: thank you Paul Newhouse, M.D., and affable assistant, Lois Casavant. Cync Psyche Credit should also go to Herbie, of Noyes Tire, who maneuvered the budget-possible purchase of "CarBaby," my alter ego, '94 Chrysler LeBaron GTC convertible,

For keeping me physically fit, thank you Dr. Donna Powell, and M.D.'s C. Irwin, R. & D. Millay, and F. Landry; to audiologist Dinah Smith of the Luse Center; Gary and Melanie of The Optical Center; and Stone Soup, where grand seigneurs Rifkin and Elliot preside beside their quick-on-the-quip staff of capital chefs.

A salute all her own to Jane Bertoni, whose careful critique played a significant part in refining the manuscript.

As for Ron Manganiello, can I ever properly express my gratitude for his precise expertise in resolving unending calls of "HELP!" with my continuing computer calamities? His calm during my crises replicates a Buddhist Rimpoche.

In closing, I preform a grateful Yoga Mudra (the Symbol of Yoga) to Virginia (with Sir John, as corollary clause) Aldrich, Judy Beals, and Ruth Polumbo. Together we received our yoga teacher certificates from Kripalu in 1994. Together we remain a good-natured quartet of unselfconscious, spiritual allies.

Bless all and each of the above. Thank you. May your lives be long, happy, healthy!

CONTENTS

(Front and Pack Pages Photography and Design: Rosel Froelich Stone)

YOGA IN THE MORNING, MARTINI AT NIGHT
or
The First Three-Score and Ten are the Hardest

"   .Is Magnificent!"

xxiii

PROLOGUE

(Rachel Anna Winfield)

It was hard for me to think of something to say for my assigned prologue in my grandmother's book. The pressure was on to come up with something pithy, relevant, telling and witty. (Grandmother aside #1: Oh, Rachel! Did I **really** issue such an imperious directive!) A tall order, to be sure.

So I sat down to put pen to paper, hoping my Pilot Precise Extra Fine would spill out an opening worthy of Yoga a.m./Martini p.m. However, much to my disappointment, it was not inclined to offer any such thing. Instead of trying to achieve the aforementioned wit and pith, then, I would like to offer the following, which may or may not come close to such a lofty objective, but which clumsily (Grandmother aside #2: No way, Rachel, can you

ever be clumsy – in writing, behavior or demeanor!) introduces the forthcoming page:

The proclamations, anecdotes, revelations, and recommendations proffered in my grandmother's narrative are ideas with which I have been acquainted my whole life, via letters, phone conversations, in-person recitations, and postcards (I can't tell you how many postcards!). So, when first I read her manuscript, it did not seem remarkable. But, upon further reflection, it occurred to me that, in fact, my grandmother's stamina, optimism, unflagging strength to press on, and good-old-fashioned gumption are truly impressive and inspiring.

Her mantra of Old Is Magnificent appears to be most resolutely true, particularly if she is the example. The poster child (or should I say "poster elder?") for being Old and Magnificent. Especially Magnificent.

So, Grandma, go ahead and tell the world what you've been telling me forever, and what I can see from your smile is unquestionably good advice.

INTRODUCTION

Focusing on the eyes of the gray owl by my window, a treasured gift from more treasured friend, I bring my attention to full awareness. Standing as tall as my five foot, one inch height allows, I raise my right leg, knee bent. I place the heel of my right foot in the palm of my right hand. Concentrated and committed, I extend the leg high in front of me with my left arm stretched straight to the side at shoulder level. For approximately fifteen seconds, I remain still. Then slowly release the hold, bend the knee again, and place my foot back on the floor. After several long breaths, I repeat the exercise with my left leg.

Twelve years ago, the mere suggestion that I might try such a feat would have blown my septuagenarian mind. Twelve years ago I was a mess: My body was continuing to age, and an operation which had removed two pieces of my spine did not make me a likely chorus-line candidate.

M.D.'s stated I would never walk properly again. My spirit had deteriorated so completely that I had twice tried suicide.

Today, I blow my now octogenarian mind as I perform the leg exercise in conjunction with a 20-40 minute routine of Kripalu Yogic stretches, breathing and meditation. I teach yoga to "The Minimums" (3-8 year olds), and "The Maximums" (those over 60). At eighty-two, I am in my prime and grow "primer" yearly.

In the main, credit goes to several close friends and one insightful psychiatrist. It could not have been easy, especially for my steadfast daughter and son. I do take credit, however, for having the sense to (1) keep at it, (2) take a chance, (3) hang on to laughter, especially at myself and (4) not give up despite the certainty that "nobody loves me. Everybody hates me. I'm going into the garden to eat worms."

Thus I repeat: I am in my prime!

How's this possible?

Let's go back to the summer of 1969 when I was fifty-one. My daughter, two companions, and I climbed the Swiss Alps. As the oldest and least sturdy, I found the going increasingly arduous, often precarious. When we reached snow, I sat down on a sun-warmed rock to proclaim my unwillingness to continue.

Madeleine placed her hands on my shoulders. Her challenge rang full and clear: "Can this be my Mom! **My** Mom with that boundless Lehman energy everyone boasts about!" She took my hand to pull me upright. "It's only a little further …."

… and only a little further, we rounded a craggy boulder to come upon the fabled Valley of Flowers. In awed immobility, we stared at the dazzling blend of violet, red, yellow, orange, white, stretching limitlessly toward a cloudless horizon. Cornflowers, cosmos, dahlias, anemones, gentians, marigold … we could not count their variety nor give them all names; we could only flop in their midst to share in silence the resonance vibrating between us. The miracle of that day, sealed in memory, sustains me still.

Twenty-two years later at age seventy-three in fall 1991, eighteen strangers and I were on the mat cautiously bending and stretching as an encouraging young man introduced us to yoga in a class at Kripalu Yoga and Health Center in Lenox, MA.

Again with urging from my daughter, I had enrolled in the Center as a desperate last resort to the dead-end discussions, readings, participatory up-lift sessions and pep-talks on the entire depressing reality of growing old, useless, ugly. I looked, pushed myself a little further and found a bright new penny of a Carol.

No matter that she represents the epitome of a Late Bloomer or Slow Starter. In fact, that's the best part, because it took her so long to come out of it, cannot this book prove to any and everyone regardless of age or physical or financial condition that it is never too late?

My years contain their share of triumph/tragedy, ecstasy/despair. While sensitive to and respectful of the tenuous fragility of age, those years allow me to suggest that the solemnity we insist upon accumulating over time accomplishes nothing in the end. No merit accompanies the dour judgments we pile upon ourselves and others. Yes, life is indeed deadly serious, especially since one day we will find ourselves seriously dead. Even though each generation walks in its own special glory, it can and should learn from the ones before.

Hence, though this book concentrates on OLD's story, and how it profits from the past, with its telling, **I want to tear up forever the paper-tiger anxiety about aging that those behind --particularly the 34 to 64 year Baby Boomers– so apprehensively await.** I want to show that, despite being eighty-two, in need of ever stronger glasses,

CHAPTER ONE: OLD IS MAGNIFICENT

The ancient Greek philosopher Plato and the modern educator Mortimer Adler span millenniums to declare in unison: not until one is into the sixties can real knowledge and wisdom be attained. Audacious Eighties Me adds: "Without that knowledge and wisdom, the flame of happiness cannot become fully realized." Not for a moment do I trivialize the power of youth's vibrant involvement. I suggest, however, that when OLD views a sunset filtered through years of sunset-viewing, it reverberates with heightened sensitivity and tenderness.

Without question youth bestrides the world with enviable vigor, reveling in its ingenuous early discoveries of joy, laughter, celebration. Yet! And Yet! They cannot know, nor can any of us know, until we find ourselves dead-ended against the implacable wall of antiquity what unsuspected enchantment awaits our epilogue --when we give it the chance.

In the 1960s, "Black Is Beautiful!" rang legitimately through the air. In the year 2000, I offer an equally legitimate cry: "Old Is Magnificent!" America fixates on youth. I often wonder what becomes of models who are has-beens at twenty-five! I shudder when reading about face lifts, body tucks, nose jobs, hair implants being performed on both women and men scarcely out of their twenties. Examine *Vogue, Elle, Esquire, Ebony.* Leaf through *Gentlemen's Quarterly, People,* even *Forbes* or *Architectural Digest.* While the photographs certainly reveal individuals of irresistible allure, do we not also spy shadows of conformity?

OLD, on the other hand, cannot stop maturing into individualized separateness. As pointed out by John W. Rowe, M.D. and Robert L. Kahn, Ph.D. in their book, *Successful Aging,* (Pantheon Books, 1998) and based upon a ten-year MacArthur Foundation Study, " . . . as no two people are alike, so too, the functional capacity of their major organs varies dramatically and tends to increase substantially with age . . . the older people become, the more dissimilar they become. If you have seen one old person, you have not seen them all. We must fight the tendency to overgeneralize about the health and abilities of older people."

How dare we OLD debase, belittle our glorious originality; try to operate, or hide it away! During my recent stint as an Extra for the Jim Carrey movie, *Me, Myself and Irene*, a stunningly handsome Screen Actors

Guild (SAG) Extra sent me into table-pounding dismay when he spoke of "having my eyes done when the first bags appear." I took him to be in his late thirties and knew he played featured though not famous roles in summer theater and other Off Broadway productions. I protested his lack of pride in self.

"But our jobs depend upon a youthful appearance. If we want good ones, we must keep looking young!"

All listening SAG members agreed emphatically. I concede it may be thus. I refuse to believe it *must* be thus! Being a first class actor does not depend upon looks. I wouldn't call Dustin Hoffman or Danny Devito drop-dead, matinee idols. Yet through the force of their belief in themselves as capable performing artists not physical paragons, they have become envied idols whose endurance will leave behind many matinee types! Look at nearing-ninety Uta Hagen, a stunning presence on stage, as is Brian Dennehy and Dame Judy Dench. Heavens! Old paintings, old crystal, even old Mickey Mouse watches have become prized possessions. Why not, then, the old among us?

The story of Mrs. Sue Reiner and her table illustrates the point:

As the young couple, Brenda and Jonathan Wilton who had recently bought Sue Reiner's home came to make a final inspection, they continually exclaimed over her taste, especially attracted by one table in particular.

"Yes. It is lovely, isn't it. I'm going to miss it when I move. I'm giving it to my daughter."

"Giving it!" Brenda's outraged voice rose with her dark eyebrows. "Surely, Mrs. Reiner, you realize that table could be taken for a Nakashima. It's so like one we saw in the Metropolitan in New York last month. We'll buy it from you right now, if you want!"

"Is that so!" Sue ran her fingers across the bruises on its dark surface, then jauntily turned to the young couple.

"Mrs. Wilton, Mr. Wilton. . ." Her diction was precise. 'That's not **like** a Nakashima, it **is** a Nakashima, George Nakashima!" She thumped her cane "That old table . . . ? A lifetime of sweet and sour reminiscences right here."

"My husband and I were so young, so impatient to furnish our home handsomely. We had seen two of his pieces at the home of friends and been overwhelmed. We made an appointment to visit his studio in New Hope, Pennsylvania, and against our strict-budget-judgment, bought that little table --just like that!!" Sue snapped her fingers and smiled as the happiness of the day reflected in her voice.

"In the midst of packing our purchase, Mr. Nakashima stopped to rap a tattoo on the table top. 'My furniture is built to endure, built to grow more handsome the more it is used. Furniture should be lived with. A certain amount of scratching, denting, adds character. A Nakashima Table becomes part of the family. You don't abuse it, but you don't spoil it, either. There's nothing quite so uninteresting as an unmarred surface that looks as if it had never been used. My tables acquire character with age, become more beautiful. . .as do people.'"

She stopped as tears misted her eyes. "Now Tim is dead, and George Nakashima, too, but I have my memories."

"You do, you do, Mrs. Reiner." Jonathan cupped her arthritic hand in his, "The Museum pieces overwhelmed us too, their unblemished elegance; but I get Nakashima's meaning. Your table has developed a special grace, like you, grown lovely!"

"Oh thank you. Even more, thank you for making me think twice about giving it away when I move. I believe I'll hang onto it as long as I live and then give it to my daughter." She clapped her hands for attention: "In ten years, ten thousand dollars won't buy it! We'll age together, together increase our value, exactly as Nakashima-san had planned."

"Right on!" Brenda raised her hand in salute. "You're awesome, Mrs. Reiner. Way to go!"

Way to go, indeed, equating Sue with her table and giving OLD its respectful due!

Prudence inspires the reminder that faster than the proverbial speeding bullet, today's young end as tomorrow's old. Courtesy bestows the right to reveal an unacknowledged secret: with age comes freedom, a freedom impossible for either youth or middle years to imagine. We attain autonomy, actually, a far more accurate word brought to my attention in a sermon by Gary Kowalski, the incisive Minister of the Burlington Unitarian-Universalist Church. "Autonomy carries more force being self-motivated."

I looked the word up. As usual, the reverend had hit the mark. It stems from "auto"-self; "nom"-law. Being autonomous permits OLD to devise laws for itself over which OLD has control. More and more, we recognize our refreshing autonomy and practice it with our practiced hands!

I put *Webster, Roget*, the *O.E.D., Random House*, the entire lot on notice. Laying no claim whatsoever to lexicographic credentials, I respectfully request them to redefine "old," as synonym for freedom, autonomy, wisdom; even a distinctive form of love, of sex.

Don't kid yourself. OLD in no way relinquishes the heady fire of sexual exhilaration. The September-October 1999 issue of *Modern Maturity* deals with sex. As an opener, Elliot Carlson, Acting Editor, writes: "The results are fascinating. As you will see, the findings affirm that sexual vitality does not necessarily lessen in later life; indeed, it may actually become richer and more complex." Let me run that by you again, "richer and more complex."

To press the point, let's hear from Nobel Laureate for Literature author Isaac Bashevis Singer, writing an author's note for his short story, *Old Love:* "Literature has neglected the old and their emotions. The novelists never told us that in life as in other matters, the young are just beginners and that the art of loving matures with age and experience."

The novelists also fail to tell us that with age comes a selective, aesthetic charisma awaiting discovery. Thus, while redefining old let us include the special beauty **only** OLD attains. "There is little character or loveliness in the face of someone who has avoided suffering, shunned risk, and rejected life," wrote Madeleine L'Engle about her mother in her book *Two Part Invention,* (Farrar, Straus & Giraux, 1988).

OLD must be affirmed, not diminished into demeaning affectations such as Senior Citizen, Mature Adult, Frail Elderly. The terminology straight-walks into the Who-Needs-It-Division of those unable to call a spade precisely that! Often and oftener people exclaim: "You're not old. You're so young in heart," believing they have given me a supreme compliment.

Young in heart is not a compliment. My childhood raises few genial memories. Nothing could persuade me to return to those young-in-heart years. Far too frequently today I meet youngsters in bitter despair. Teen age suicide rises in scary numbers. Only last week, a twenty-three-year old Adonis told me: "I'm confused. I can't figure life . . . other guys, ya' know, feel the same. Then we look at you, how old you are. . . yet peaceful, seeming to understand . . ."

We are more peaceful. We do understand. That's what longevity is all about, and it will not stand up to stereotyping.

When people say "you don't look eighty-two," I can only counter, "But I am eighty-two! This is what eighty-two looks like!" When they proclaim "your spirit is so

11

youthful! ," my answer continues, "it's an eighty-two spirit! No youngster can possibly feel this ebullient. First, ya gotta **get** old!" I even meet elementary school students whose depression alarms me. When I come upon their happier peers, I want to say "**you** remind me of an eighty-year-old!" Now **that's** a compliment.

Robert N. Butler, M.D., founder and former director of the Department of Geriatrics at Mt. Sinai Medical Center and now Chairman of the Mt. Sinai Gerald and May Ellen Ritter Department of Geriatrics and Adult Development, maintains: "Age is a triumph, not a burden. Age has nothing to do with anything. Attitude does."

And with the arrival of 2000, comes a revelation from the Science Section of *The New York Times* of Tuesday, January 4, under Sandra Blakeslee's byline: "As scientists look back at the discoveries of the 1990's, one finding stands out as the most startling, and most difficult to accept; people are *not* born with all their brain cells. .

.Mature circuits appear to be maintained by *new cell growth* (italics mine) well into old age!"

SAG performers, everyone! Instead of waging war **against** your bodies with medications or painful operations, rise up in arms to enfold them in increasing self respect and esteem. Beauty and brains accompany you still. The major trick revolves around acknowledging them with confidant assurance. Not easy. Not easy at all. Yet -- try this on for size:

A peaches-and-cream-complected young beauty recently walked into The Body Shop where I am a part time salesperson. She started to try on make-up. "Oh! **What** am I to **do** about these lines around my eyes! I'm an absolute disaster!" Her grimace of self-disgust astonished me.

"Are you for **real**," I almost shouted in my dismay at her evaluation. "I saw you come in. I thought now 'that one's beyond reproach!'" I walked toward her. "You want lines, look at me! **These** are lines." I pointed to five or six exceptionally deep ones. "But they've become friends. I've decided they make me beautiful!"

"They do. They **should** be friends!." She flashed a smile as she gave me a critical once-over. "On you they look good. On me they're awful, simply awful! Scares me to death how I'm getting old!"

Ah-HA! On the instant we are presented with The Perfect Paradox Paradigm for this book: So consumed was the lovely young woman with misconceptions about aging, she could not recognize how those very lines bestowed a quality to her face that served as the **basis** for her special beauty. The obsessive fear of old had blinded not only her common sense but obvious fact. And yet, in complete self-contradiction, she beholds my long- **long**-ago-gotten-old face and readily acclaim **its** beauty!

People have become so afraid of an aging body they are unable to acknowledge its distinctive charm when they run smack into it. The time has come for Old Affirmation! Start now. Convince yourself that life's inevitable changes bring on dazzling individuality. You will become transformed as will those around you.

Beauty, runs the cliche, is in the eye of the beholder! Like most cliches, it rings loud with truth. I have become friends with my lined face and gnarled hands, recognizing that they lend me signature elegance.

The statement sinuously segues into an explanation of why I capitalize OLD. I do this to emphasize my new definition and re-evaluation: OLD serves as acronym for "**O**bvious **L**ife **D**ecisions." Being alive grants us personal freedom either to *let* things happen or *make* things happen. Will we don our distinctive mantel of brains and beauty or submissively hand it over to a younger generation? It is our choice to assume an *active* or *passive* voice; to make our own **O**bvious **L**ife **D**ecisions.

For me, yoga gave me the necessary boost. Now that I practice regularly and teach others, I grow increasingly confident and cheerful, especially with my guiltless evening martini. (Note: martini is singular. Two and I would not be able to practice morning yoga!)

After reading Chapter Two, " Zeroing In," I offer the subsequent five as guidelines to help you on your way. I hope you will try them.

Chapter Three: Be an angel, take yourself lightly!

Chapter Four: Adopt I.W.N.B.V. (I Will Not Be Victimized)

Chapter Five: Grab the fringe benefits

Chapter Six: Be good to yourself

Chapter Seven: Why Yoga. Why Martini

The hard work in the beginning, before the disciplines become reassuring habits, results in exhilarating success that increases exponentially. Of course your beauty and your brains undergo a metamorphosis, but they certainly survive – triumphantly!

I'll prove it to you if you're game to try.

Let's get to work!

CHAPTER TWO: ZEROING IN

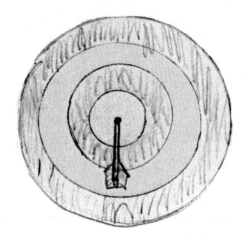

Fear and apology represent OLD's harshest enemy! This chapter, therefore, is dedicated to the valiant, Over Sixty, Day-By-Day Survivors who repudiate such self-fulfilling prophecies to face with determined confidence the Fact of OLD.

Familiar we are with achievers whose remote lives often minimize our own: Benjamin Franklin at 81 affecting the compromise that saved our Constitution; Michelangelo still creating masterpieces at 88; Mike Wallace, Dr. Seuss, Pete Seeger, octogenarians all. The list moves onto nonagenarians: Comedian Bob Hope; Painter Georgia O'Keeffe; dancer-choreographers Agnes DeMille and Merce Cunningham, then to the most awesome of all, potter Beatrice Wood still at work when she died at 105.

The powerful momentum of their genius compelled them to endure. Assuredly they stand out as OLD IS MAGNIFICENT! models. To justify my crusade, however, we need examples of ordinary people aging into **ex**traordinary people with**out** portfolios.

Eva Sharper

Married in her early twenties, she mothered five children, burying two and a husband. Though not moneyed or educated, she was, like most women of her era, wise to the ways of the world and possessed of a dazzling flare for embroidery. She survived five major operations, despite one in 1955 that had the doctors giving up on any possible recovery.

A decade ago, her son, Donald, organized a celebration to honor her birthday. Many well-wishers had spent several hours wishing her well. She and I, sitting slightly apart from the revelers, enjoyed watching and commenting, sometimes artfully, about their antics. At one point, she let out a sigh and leaned back in her chair. I grew concerned and turned to her. "Aren't all these enthusiastic guests and activities wearing you down? Shouldn't I take you upstairs to rest?

A tall woman, Eva Sharper looked at me, her back growing stiff. "What makes you think I'm tired!" Her indignant riposte made my back **tingle.** "And if I were, don't you think I have the sense to say so!" It was not a question. "I enjoy the attention! I know how lucky I am to have a son like Donald." The delivery hit with staccato firmness. "I hope he continues celebrating my anniversaries. I enjoy living."

Where had I dropped my head? --or heart, for that matter? What did I, could I, know about this woman beside me, closing in on a century of living? What right had I to assume --because she was old-- she couldn't decide for herself if she needed to rest? Eva Sharper died a few months before her 100th birthday. I do not forget her nor the incisive lesson she taught me.

Maggie Smith

Maggie Smith had lived in a wheelchair in a nursing home in St. Johnsbury, Vermont for twenty years. She participated in a painting program, G.R.A.C.E. (Vermont's **G**rass **R**oots **A**rt **a**nd **C**ommunity **E**ffort), inaugurated by the distinguished artist, Don Sunseri of Glover. Under his guidance, she became a first-rate primitive artist whose work has become collector material.

21

Interviewing Maggie Smith for a newspaper article, I suggested readers would be interested in her attitude about aging. "You always seem upbeat! Surely you go through periods of depression, anger, even!"

Maggie Smith's patrician face wrinkled into an almost imperceptible smile as she considered the statement. Slowly, she looked around the room. My gaze followed hers across to the other mostly silent and in some way disabled men and women. "Oh, don't let this ever happen to me," I moaned silently. "This isn't any way to live!

As if I had spoken, Maggie Smith reached forward with one of her painter hands, forcing me to look directly at her. "Of course we grow discouraged." The power of her voice held my attention. "We talk of ways to end it, of how we wish we had greater control of our own lives, resentful of the rules here." Her eyes would not leave mine. Her tone grew in strength. "Some of us --not me, fortunately-- have thoughtless family wanting to take over every detail of our lives. Before Don and his program came here, I even began hiding sleeping pills, trying to figure how many I would need, but they catch on, watch us too closely."

She turned her head away, perhaps embarrassed by the confession. "But Don did come. His program made a dramatic difference to many of us. I became excited about my painting. It made me remember how life had been with Paul. It's fifteen years since he died." She brushed aside a strand of hair. "As you know, living in rural Vermont is not easy even now. It was worse then! Sometimes, in evenings by the wood stove, we'd look at each other asking if it was worth it, back then fifty years ago . . . " She looked around the room, waving her hand slightly as if wanting to include the others in her words: "That's important, 'worth it!' We talk about it all the time. It seems, despite wheelchairs, pain, the nursing home, our aloneness, most of us most of the time continue to believe it **is** worth it." She was so concentrated on expressing herself properly that she did not notice the woolen shawl slipping from her bony knees. "Maybe I have no right saying this, but I believe it **takes** being old to recognize completely how precious life is. Young people -- how old are you?" "Sixty-seven!" "Well, yes, even young like you!" We exchanged smiles of acknowledgment at the thirty years separating us. "You cannot appreciate how tenaciously we cling to life. How . . . well . . . sacred it becomes." Surprised by her intensity, she lowered her gaze, spied the shawl and placed it carefully back on her knees. "Here I am at ninety-six with a new profession, in some way happier than ever!"

Franz Kafka's *Reflections* came to mind: "You do not need to leave your room. Remain at your table and listen. Do not even listen, simply wait, be quite still and solitary. The world will freely offer itself to you to be unmasked, it has no choice, it will roll in ecstasy at your feet."

Mr. Hertsfield, Herzfeld, Hartsfeld

His right leg swung in a stiff semicircle. The cane in his knobbed hand thumped a slow tread on the Boardwalk at Asbury Park in New Jersey, where he walked early in the morning every day of summer, rain or shine. "That's the time to see the birds, hear their calls clearly, watch them swoop and soar, scramble like-wind-up toys across the sand."

Mr. Hertsfield, Herzfeld, Hartsfeld (I never did catch his name precisely) and I joined our measured steps together. The morning breeze riffled his abundantly gray-white curls but his face seemed a flotsam, seaweed reflection of our surroundings. Not a robust man, yet able to march with impressive determination, we connected comfortably, the two of us and the birds, as strangers often do on trains or ships or early morning encounters by the sea. Our talk, as opposed to our walk, rambled at a leisurely pace. Bit by bit, pieces of his life revealed themselves.

Recently widowed after fifty-one years of happy marriage, he continued to summer in their waterfront home in Deal and wintered in their east side Brownstone in New York. One child, a hopelessly retarded daughter lived in a special home he visited once a week. How easily he could have retreated in self-pity behind the walls of his obviously comfortable solitude. Not **this** Hertzfeld, Herzfield, Hartsfeld. He was matriculating at Columbia University, studying for a doctorate in ornithology. "I want to teach poor kids about birds. Take them to the Audubon Society, to Central Park, to the sanctuaries surrounding the city. Studying birds fills my heart, makes me less lonely. Whatever time's left to me, that's where my energies will go."

Arms resting on the rail, we looked across the ocean expanse, convinced that the aging student would attain his goal. He understood that bogey word, OLD just as had

Eva Sharper and Maggie Smith. Each as worthy OLD IS MAGNIFICENT! models as any celebrities.

How did they achieve their magnificence? What made **them** able to fight, keep fighting despite decreasing health? What makes me, for that matter?

"Stay active! "Keep involved," cry the cries from pulpit, class room, and scholarly tome after tome after tome. Great! Smart thinking! Good advice! But **how,** and **why** and **wherefore** can some follow the advice while others sink into a slough of despond? I am not convinced there is a definitive answer. I **am** convinced that learning from the lives of others will give a jump start.

I know nothing about the childhoods of Eva, Maggie or Herzfeld. I do, however, know mine. Though it tears skin from nerves, if I am to establish authenticity for my peaceful present, I must revitalize those buried, psychic scars and place them in the Forget-Forgive Department.

The product of an eminently respected private girl's school and camp my parents owned and directed, introduced early to all the arts, including opera, the graduate of a first rate woman's college, mine was an enviable cultural and educational environment, even to the comforts of wealth--chauffeur, gardener, cook, maid, governess. I had it all, didn't I?

My mother had a chum, Aunt Harriet (we bestowed the honorific aunt or uncle on all adult friends then), who walked everywhere. Ahead of her time, Aunt Harriet knew all about remaining active, striding three to five miles a day across the streets of New York City right up to her death at seventy-three.

An independent woman of principles as rigid and firm as her back, she was the only one I ever knew to question father. A distinguished 1902 graduate of Yale University and director of a prestigious college preparatory school, father strode across his small   domain as acknowledged Man of Distinction. ·

One afternoon when I was nine, he and Aunt Harriet became involved in a heated disagreement over a grammatical phrase in my history book. Each grew redder and angrier. Even though their voices never rose above a somber alto, I sensed their controlled rage.

"Stop!   Please! Please!   Stop!" I leapt from the protecting, upholstered chair, pushing myself between them. Realizing they had forgotten me, they grew instantly silent. Harriet took a breath, "Oh Carol. How sorry I am! Of course it scared you! I can see how upsetting it can be having   someone confront your father, disagreeing with him, especially a woman."

"That   will be enough, Harriet," he enforced the directive by pointing a finger to the door. "Leave! Leave immediately!"

With characteristic straight back, she lifted her long skirt just enough to assure a defiant exit. I turned toward father who had obviously dismissed the episode as a non-event. He chuckled, winking at me as if we shared a delicious secret. "Don't let this upset you, Baby Girl. It means nothing, really, nothing. We must learn to forgive Harriet when she has these little, female tantrums." He winked again. "That's why she behaves unwisely from time to time and requires being called to task. She doesn't have money, either, and therefore must support herself by teaching public school."

I stared at my tartan skirt, lining up its pleats as if my life depended upon it. For the first time in my life I didn't want to listen to him. "Teaching younger grades is a worthy profession for a woman, and I haven't a doubt she does a first rate job." He tilted my chin. I had to look at him. To listen. "Fortunately, **you'll** never be in such a situation." He laughed lightly. "You not only have me, but

30

two older brothers." He kissed my cheek, "and you're such a pretty Baby Girl the boys will come flocking around in later years." With that he left the room, as if nothing more needed to be said.

Lot's more did, though. I adored Aunt Harriet. To me she seemed happier than Auntnie, the pet name we had given our cherished Aunt Estelle, Mother's older sister who lived with us. We had great fun when she came to visit, introducing us to books like *The Wizard of Oz*, or the poetry of Ogden Nash. She imitated people with such skill, mother would chide, "Oh Harriet, you shouldn't," even as she joined our laughter.

That night at bedtime, I spoke to mother about the fight, asked her if father was right. Mother, amid all manner of roiled household waters managed, like her favorite bird the loon, to sail across them with serene detachment. Slender and fragile though she was, her mere presence brought comfort. "Your father is always right, Carol." Her tranquil

31

assurance eased my confusion. "Aunt Harriet is an unusual woman of ability and character. Our friendship is important to us both. Don't ever think ill of her, but Daddy is correct. She isn't married, she doesn't understand men, the importance of catering to their needs first, especially to a husband as important as your father." She kissed me on the forehead. She smelled of lavender, she always smelled of lavender. "You're too young to talk of this today. But when you're older . . . the time will come before we know it." She kissed me again, whispered, "I love you. Goodnight."

The time did not come. Shortly thereafter, mother became fatally ill. Ambulances screamed to and from the house bringing her to a hospital for months, then carrying her home for longer periods to be confined in her room unable to have visitors except on rare occasions. Mother as mother had disappeared.

During her illness of about five years, she dealt uncomplainingly with increasingly painful cancer and diabetes. A gentlewoman of poetry and flowers, she remained steadfast in her courage. I would visit her at the hospital, a pale, white lily unable to ruffle the bed covering. But the lily's yellow center smiled sunshine at my every visit.

How she must have suffered! She had both cancer and diabetes. Medicine knew little then about either illness. I tremble still remembering one fatal day soon after her return home from the hospital after a massive mastectomy operation. I knocked gently on the bedroom door but received no answer. Tentatively, I opened it and peeked in. I cried out upon seeing what I later learned was a blood transfusion, a medical procedure performed at home in those days.

There lay Mother and Father, fully dressed, stretched side-by-side, flat out on top of the bed surrounded by bottles, syringes and tubes entangled in veined, naked arms. In terror, I stared as two nurses and a doctor towered over them. I must have cried out again, because they turned to descend angrily upon me, shoving me from the door. "Get out. Get OUT! You have no business in here."

Later, my timid questions were brushed aside. "You're too young, much too young to understand. Just put it out of your mind, forget it!"

I was not too young for continuing nightmares and definitely old enough so that even now I cannot forget.

For those final five years of her life, Mother had been so frequently either hospitalized or secluded in her room that I rarely saw her. She became an ephemeral presence, an untouchable, porcelain figure of such fragility that during our brief visits, I hesitated to kiss her. Until Mother, no one close to me had died. Thus, her death when I turned thirteen, had no immediate impact. I hadn't an inkling of its finality nor did I understand the reason for the tumultuous turnaround in my beautiful home and its well-ordered routine.

I watched in dry-eyed confusion as people known and unknown swept passed me as if I were invisible. Years earlier, due to a fight over money, Auntnie and Aunt Harriet, who had taken her side, had been ordered "out of the house, never to return." Because of that commandment, those two precious allies were not on hand to explain or comfort me. My brothers must have returned for the funeral, but I have no memory of grieving with them. Father came and went, surrounded by women I did not know, fawning on him, pushing me aside even as they issued directives apparently from him regarding the routine I was expected to follow.

People around me were crying, but I didn't, even at the funeral. Even after seeing her resting in the coffin, it didn't sink in. She had been made up exquisitely. Her face was filled with a color on her cheeks I hadn't seen in years. She looked beautiful in her pale blue ball gown and rope pearl necklace. Am I right remembering she even had on her favorite, silver, pearl-buttoned dancing pumps? Through all those months, I failed to come to grips either in my head or heart with what dead meant. Dead, done for, gone. It did not register. . . until four months later.

We were at the handsome, oak dinner table in our formal dining room. Father sat in his customary place at its head. But presiding imperiously where my gentle mother should have been, sat my Aunt Dodo. I didn't know why. She and Uncle Louis, who in past years only showed up for holidays, were shadow figures in my life. Shadow figures I tried to avoid. They had no children of their own and I felt they were very glad of that fact.

But now, in mother's place sat sour-faced Aunt Dodo. I stared at her serving the food. And it hit me! Really, truly grabbed at my gut Mother would never, never-never-ever sit there again. I slammed down the linen napkin and jumped up so fast, I spilled the water glass. I rushed from the room screaming, screaming with such terror, the sound merely increased my terror: "She's **not** coming back. Mother's NEVER coming back!" I ran to the living room, flinging myself onto the huge upholstered chair. Aunt Dodo followed. "Isn't it a bit **late** for tears, Carol? What are you after? Where were your tears when she died or at her funeral?"

A witch, I decided, with all that fluffed red hair massed loosely about her face, a few actually sticking out of her nose and chin. "You want us all to concentrate on **you**, as if only you counted."

Uncle Louis had followed Aunt Dodo: "What's her problem?"

"Problem? The child wants attention, that's the problem. Well, she'll see that such unbecoming table manners won't get her anywhere." Out they walked, a cement condemnation I could not smash. I just sat

37

watching, all by myself, waiting for a father who never came. I sank against the chair, sobs easing, misery growing.

My isolation grew with whirlwind force as our gracious home and garden mutated into metallic business offices. The imposing dining room with its carved oak table that could seat twenty evaporated to be replaced by desks, files, typewriters, and telephones. The spacious living room with its thick Persian carpet transformed itself overnight into austere offices for bookkeepers and their equipment.

I lived at home, not with students in the dorms. At day's end when I returned, no longer was I met with smiles and cookies and warm embraces from Annie, our cook or Archie, the chauffeur, sitting comfortably in the huge, sunny kitchen. No, now I walked into business offices. If I said hello to the staff, they returned my greetings with an impersonal nod and the suggestion that "you go upstairs to your room and get busy with your homework."

Up I would go. Shut the door and turn on"Myrt and Marge," or other afternoon radio shows, burying my face in King, "Kingie," my magnificent-maned collie.

I dared not go into Father's office. During the day he remained aloof and unapproachable. I rarely saw him except for our unnerving, good night "games" that were all-too intimate for me to feel relaxed or comfortable about. Yet, at least during those times I had his complete attention. Raised in Puritan ignorance, I failed to admit, much less come to terms with, the full consequences of his behavior until well beyond maturity. In fact, black forgetfulness so encompassed me that I was in my forties before admitting them into remembrance. I had told no one, not my husband, friends, no one.

But even those bewildering bedtimes ended abruptly when, without previous explanation, Florence Chase, her husband Sam, and young sister Elisabeth materialized in full possession of our spacious third floor apartment where my brothers had lived before going off to boarding school and college.

Father's succinct explanation for the sudden arrival of these three strangers taking over so authoritatively came out in three declarative sentences: "Florence, an educated, intelligent woman will become Social Director, assuming responsibilities much like those your mother once performed. Sam, an expert on business management, will serve in that capacity. Elizabeth will be my personal secretary."

From that point on, not only did my evenings with father end, but this Elizabeth began to control my life. It was awful. Just awful. She treated me like a baby. She went through my closets and bureau drawers, making decisions as to whether or not I needed clothing. She screened phone calls and told me when I could have visitors in my room. On several occasions she actually ordered friends out of the room, and once I came upon her at my desk reading my personal mail. When I complained, father, he countered with a cavalier, "If you are behaving yourself and have nothing to hide what difference does it make? Elizabeth is a very wise woman. She will keep you from making foolish errors as you mature."

To compound matters, I never felt bonded to my schoolmates because of our separate living quarters. They, there together in the dormitory, me going home each night. As the Director's Daughter, I couldn't convince them I would not carry home tales. I tried, but when secrets or complaints were exchanged, it was behind my back Even little complaints.

One afternoon with fellow classmates Shirley and Phyllis, I spent an hour bicycling around and around The Oval, as we called the roadway circling the school campus. After an hour, we collapsed on Shirley's bed, chattering about school. Phyllis lit into Miss Patterson in English class.

"What a beast she can be. I don't know how she gets away with it!"

"Neither do I, but Dr. Lehman takes her side no matter what. There's no. . . . " Shirley clapped her hand to her mouth. "Oh, Carol. I forgot you're here. You'll tell on us, won't you?"

"Never. Believe me, I promise, cross my heart. Hope to die. I won't **ever** say a word."

They didn't believe me. Just changed the subject as conversation came to a halt. I went home, dejected, rejected. Here again, I faced another example of how normal relationships seemed impossible. I was always, apart and alone.

Though the wary acceptance that separated me from fellow students hurt, in some ways, even worse was the constant, critical eyes of teachers, secretaries, even grounds keepers waiting to pounce. I was expected to be on best behavior, continually On Display. I could not commit even a minor infraction of rules.

Once in sixth grade, I came home chewing gum A secretary grabbed my arm, leading me toward father's office. "How dare you chew gum . . . in this house? The director's daughter! You know it's forbidden."

Father scowled when told of my disobedience. "Carol. You represent the school, me. We expect more from you. It may seem unfair, but that's the way it is."

I never felt safe, able to relax. I trusted no one, and I guess no one trusted me. Two Carols existed side-by-side, equally evanescent, neither real. One Carol maintained a happy face, never daring to complain whether at home or at school and always struggling to perform perfectly, excel in class, look neat, walk properly, ever striving to please, but knowing the inevitable disapproving judge stood around the bend. The other Carol surfaced only in her room behind the closed door. There she lived an imaginary life with

King, her beautiful collie dog, as a confidante and uncritical chum. Yet even in the solitude of that room, Carol dared not let imagination go too far.

Reviewing those years, *The 2001 Space Odyssey* comes to mind. *The Beautiful Blue Danube* floated me through a tasteless, noiseless, odorless vacuum. Untroubled by gravity, I drifted from one experience to another never finding buoy or sign post by which to be guided for a place to land; randomly bumping into bewildering debris. A critical comment or forcefully delivered opinion could send me airborne in an opposite direction without a demur. Carol refused to surface; especially since the brainwashing steadily increased.

"Father says girls aren't smart enough to play chess," my brothers taunted, shooing me from the room when I asked them to teach me. Both vigorously deny the chauvinism. Loving them as I do, I allow their denials.

"Girls don't need to know math," father reassured me when I told him how frustrated I had become with algebra. "Girls aren't really talented in those fields, anyway. But **you** needn't worry your pretty head. It certainly won't be of much use to you when you're married and that day will arrive before we know it."

These burdens accompanied me through four intimidating college years. I diligently went to class, did the homework, participated in extra-curricula activities but always with a detached, impersonal attention. I managed to be graduated but did not attend the ceremony. No one from home planned to come. I certainly wasn't going to go all by myself.

My only success during those four college years was my popularity on the boy's college circuit, which back then meant more than grades. I flitted from Dartmouth to Princeton, to Harvard, Yale, Cornell, Amherst, all of them then strictly male institution as was my Alma Mater entirely female.

My lighthearted chatter and buoyant persona gave no hint of dark undercurrents I feared to face. Dishonest to myself and certainly to others, I had not the courage to look inside, express feelings or contrary opinions. I labeled myself "pretender," "phony," hoping no one would catch on. The labels followed even into my ill-starred marriage of twenty-five years. Neither Warren nor I was prepared for the responsibility.

Our courtship began on falsehoods that could not later be overcome. It wasn't my brains and beauty that held Warren initially in thrall but my father's charm and erudition. "With a Daddy like yours, and all his money, the daughter should be a real catch," he shot at me years later in one of our many, meanspirited fights. "Well! Neither came true, did it," he added bitterly. "That Elizabeth bitch and her family sure hung onto it!"

Even worse, he had wooed me straight out of Rostand's *Cyrano de Bergerac*, with a barrage of beautiful love-letters, written, it turned out, by his medical school roommate, Peter. It was those very letters that actually won me, captivating me completely. Not until Warren went overseas in World War II, sending home banal missives of simple, declarative statements, did I learn the truth. "Peter had a crush on you, and agreed to write," he told me upon his return. "I didn't realize they were that important. He probably still has a crush on you, but then, he hasn't lived with you all these years."

That story emphasizes how I disappointed him. . .and he, me. We seldom had the courage to deal honestly with one another. Both of us were afraid of intimacy. On two occasions, our clashes actually ended in his physically abusing me.

Once he beat me so severely, I required medical attention. I sought out a woman doctor from a distant county. Imagine! **I** was too ashamed of myself, **myself**, to seek a so-called, "proper" male M.D.; certainly not to one of the many who were friends. The weight of my inferiority, my guilt convinced me it was only my fault.

Looking back, no clue explains how I garnered the audacity, at age forty-four, to begin anew, seek a divorce at a time when censure frowned heavily thereon. Remember that this was pre Betty Freidan's 1963, *The Feminine Mystique.* Had it come to my attention, I'm not sure it would have helped. I can only assume I somehow amassed the guts to break away, in part because our children, Madeleine and Gregory, were in college. My wretched world had presented but one option: "Get a life!"

Veneered with bravado, I set forth to seek my fortune, circa 1961-62, just before The Feminist Movement and The Civil Rights Act emerged. Ms Unprepared Naive, I applied for my first job interview to the offices of Impresario Sol

Hurok, an experience that epitomizes those years: and all the previous decades:

Responding to my letter, Mr. Hurok's personal secretary, Daphne called. A cordial chat ended with an appointment. On the dot I appeared, hesitantly introducing myself to Marion, the exquisite young receptionist. Instead of the greeting I anticipated, she let out a cry. "You're **old!** You seemed young on the phone! You must be at least forty!" As I took in that judgment, she pressed the intercom, "Daphne, Carol Winfield's here -- but she's OLD!" Whispered words passed. The intimidating beauty gave me the once over. "In her forties!" This I heard clearly. Marion faced me. "How old **are** you?"

She relayed the mumbled "forty-four" as they resumed whispering. I picked up a magazine while unsuccessfully trying to listen in on their conversation. She released the intercom, her long, lacquered nail upon the button. "I'm sorry, Carol, I am. Daphne says there's no point in wasting her time or yours. She asked me to apologize for any inconvenience you've been through, but the Hurok office doesn't hire old women. She said to thank you for coming and to reimburse you for any expense."

Today no employer would dare risk such an observation or admit to such a policy. Back then it was a par for the course. I found myself slinking apologetically out the door, equally convinced of my unseemly oldness.

Who today equates forty-four as OLD? I write these words and don't believe them, even while knowing their truth. To me, my fifty-plus children are still children, for heavens sakes! Yet I remember one morning talking to my opera associates about an especially enjoyable date from the previous evening. One of the secretaries said to my face, "It's amazing, Carol, a woman as old as you still getting guys to take you out!" The worst part was, it amazed me, too!

Today, I cannot recognize that Carol from the past. Today, Carol holds her own beside the nameless other women and men who fought to secure these attitudes and rights everyone now takes for granted.

Any of you may justifiably call: "So what! You should have had **my** troubles!" Which is precisely my point! Rare is the individual who lives in a Rose Garden. Yet here I am, after years of doggedly developing a series of mental, spiritual, and physical disciplines that enabled me at last to acknowledge myself as a whole person --most of the time! Living primarily on Social Security, I claim residency in that illusive Garden through my credo: Acknowledge, Remember, **Forgive**!

My father was a product of **his** time, **his** culture. A learned scholar of unyielding courage and energy, he gave all three of his children the powerful will to live long, healthfully, actively. The school and camp, while Mother lived to guide him, held an unassailable reputation for

51

excellence. Mother's death dug so deep and wide a hole within the center of his being that nothing later could fill that space. The camp and school never again attained such stature.

Toward his life's end, we both mellowed. I now treasure his gifts to me. During Mother's lifetime, he brought fantasy and laughter and make-believe into our home. He enabled me to discipline myself. Whatever demons invaded him after Mother died, he rid himself of them so that during his final years, in his 80s and 90s, we spent happy times together.

I know him for a decent man, despite egregious shortcomings. I know he tried to be a good father. He came from another era, another culture. I have no right to hold bitter grudges. I feel it a blessing that I can say I am at peace with his memory.

It is the same with my husband. It was not easy dealing with schizo me. I could not have been more unprepared for domesticity. I scarcely knew how to boil water. All I knew about cooking was how to take left-over chicken out of the refrigerator to arrange it handsomely on a Balique platter. Cleaning? I knew the trade name, Dutch Cleanser, but not how to apply it. As for sewing, even today a buttonhole presents unsurmountable barriers. Always there had been servants to handle those details! Even now, except for cooking, I remain inept.

Our divorce could not have been more hateful. Accusations, recriminations flew back and forth between us and the lawyers. He didn't want to give me a penny. I wanted everything. It hurts to write these words today. It hurts, because of our later reconciliation. I dislike dredging that past. We both were able to confess our regrets, to own up to our weaknesses. We apologized to one another, became good friends. During his final illness when I lived in Vermont, he asked me to come to New Jersey to care for him. I did.

I am so glad. I have been set free. And, oh, how much easier and happier for all of us, children, grandchildren, friends, that we share memories in comfortable harmony.

A brilliant General Practitioner of character and bravery, he listened to and cared about his patients. Long before the advent of Civil Rights, he refused to distinguish patients by their color, race or religion, frequently running into trouble with hospital admissions. "Why didn't you **say** you were sending a Negro? You expect me to place him in the same room as a **white** man?" "I expect you to place him in the best room available, period." At Christmas, he invariably sent "paid in full" bills to those whose economies needed a boost. Present day physicians could profit from his hands-on, caring, intelligent attention. Sometimes, in one day he would see as many as forty patients but never rushed any through. He would come home exhausted, long after dinner hour. I know I never fully appreciated how hard he worked, how much he gave to each patient.

My life is richer and far more tranquil now because of forgiveness. I do not forget. One need not, for we learn from our past. The significant lesson evolves from the face that bad as moments may have been, good resulted. It usually does.

A smile comes to my face, remembering my sister-in-law, Florence Walls Lehman. Despite undergoing ugly divorce proceedings with my brother we remained close. Our staunch sisterhood was held together through humor and laughter. Her "Listen, Buster," forever ricochets in my ear. The phrase preceded any put down to follow. Phony nonsense never passed muster with Florence.

When we went glum, each consoled the other with the unassailable fact that, had it not been for those spouses, from whence would have cometh our superior, spectacular children, and even more of same grandchildren.

Florence came to as happy terms with my brother as did I with Warren. We let go forever of accumulated anger, rage, and bitterness and certainly lead happier lives because of that. Remember of course, but then set yourself free to acknowledge and forgive.

I had reason to hold tight to ugliness, nurturing revenge. But why? What is accomplished? The attitudes merely implode one's own joy in today. The constant calls for vengeance become internalized, gnawing irritants precluding any possible release for a soothing old age. Every one of us commits shameful follies; most of us strive for worthwhile lives; all of us deal with situations influenced by a particular time and place. The canniest of us continues to look ahead, determined to remain optimistically involved.

Robert M. Restak, M.D., writing in *Older & Wiser*, (Simon & Schuster, 1997) carefully details the effect of such an attitude on the aging brain: ". . . education is a lifetime process . . . and does not necessarily involve traditional book learning. It confers antiaging benefits. . .enhances the sense of well-being. As our performance improves as a result of our learning, we generally feel more empowered, more confident."

My delight in my age and activities are a direct result of such self-induced empowerment. I recommend the policy even to the most frail. Beyond doubt at later bloomer, I am living-breathing proof that it is never too late–or early–to bring on a physical, mental, spiritual turnabout, and seek to share, to lead you if you wish into magnificent oldness.

Read on as we move on!

CHAPTER THREE: Be an Angel, Take Yourself

Lightly

It behooves me to begin by giving credit where due.

The chapter heading has been cribbed (without permission)

from various deft rhetoricians but came first from my

mother: "Angels," she told me during one hospital visit

when I asked if she would ever come back to her own

room, "move delicately across the earth. You may think

I'm not home. But I am always with you, flying lightly

beside you even as you sleep. Be like the angels," her

silken voice urged, all too aware of her short life span, my dearest daughter, gay and bright and weightless!"

Just so. And just so for those of us on and beyond our sixth decade. We shall assume butterfly wings of angelic lightness to embody the magnificence of OLD!

The Plus Side:

Drive with me to Racquet's Edge Health Club in Essex Junction, Vermont. Observe, if you will, its Plus Side Senior Aerobics program: Led by Sheree Wellins and assisted by Jody Fiore, they reflect the zestful commitment of their students, whose age and fitness vary strikingly. Attentively working out and up a healthy sweat for their 40-60 nonstop minutes workout, students transform the room until it sparkles in simulated sunlight engendered purely by their supportive camaraderie. When class ends, they exchange anecdotes -- more often than not jokes on themselves.

Now follow me down a flight of stairs, across the hall to the aerobics for younger men and women. Watch them attentively working out and up a healthy sweat for 40-60 nonstop minutes. The instructor issues Marine Corps directives reflecting the solemn, silent concentration of these lither, younger students. At the session's conclusion, they pick up their gear, exit the room with the same isolated determination as when they had walked in. Though both groups enjoyed equal physical benefit, I would bet you a week in Bali about which class had more fun, garnered more fringe benefits.

Ditto Elder Hostel. Last summer I met three health professionals who had worked with both Club Med and Elder Hostel programs. "No contest," the 28-year-old swimmer chortled: "Give me Elder Hostel any time." Mr. Thirty-something in charge of Programming waxed beatific: "They're fun, old people. Awesome!" Ms College Junior, waitress, became belligerent: "Those   Club Med diners behaved as if 'slave' were my title while the Elder Hostels kept saying 'please' and 'thank-you;' even apologizing for a service that's part of my job! I want to help them."

Two prestigious professor friends, one of music, the other of English literature, at two prestigious universities, equate Elder Hostel classes with vacation. The Music Man: "Their curiosity and enthusiasm makes teaching a total joy. I love 'em all! " The English Professor: "Even those without a college degree seems one jump ahead of me! Often we're entangled in an intense 'who's on first' battle of wits!" Whether at school, spa or health club, OLD knows without prodding how to benefit from a light touch.

Grandfather

After the Philadelphia annual Thanksgiving Day Parade, the sky became as gray as a battered cooking pot while the cold wind turned noses of the going-home crowd into red cranberries. Ahead of us on the crowded sidewalk walked a militarily-erect, white-haired man with three children clinging to him. A fourth sat high and proud on his shoulders.

We stopped at the curb for the red light. I noticed the oldest boy, about thirteen, squeezed his grandfather's long-fingered hand while another boy about nine hung tight to the man's other hand. "Grandpa," a girl of seven or so, with rakish curls, holding the hand of her brother, peeked round from beneath a brightly colored stocking cap. "I liked the queen and her diamond tiara the very-very best." He turned his head only slightly as the tyke on his shoulders pressed mittened hands into his pointed chin. "Ms. Piggy, I liked Ms Piggy, I liked Ms Piggy best. You're gonna take us next year, aren't you Gramps, aren't you?"

"Burton, have I missed once since Adam was five?" Adam placed his arm protectively on Grandfather's elbow as we crossed the street in a group. "Nope, " he agreed, looking at his sister trying to edge her off. "Okay, Caitlin, you can change places with me. You don't need to push."

"Oh Gramps," Caitlin pressed the old man's hand to her cheek. "No one's as much fun in the whole wide world!"

We reached the curb just as two football-center sized teenagers charged from the other direction, pushing Gramps back against me. We wobbled in a precarious balance act, but remained standing. He turned, reaching toward me. "Are you hurt, " he asked, speaking so softly I almost didn't hear him.

Moving my arms vigorously back and forth I said "See! See! I'm fine, not a scratch," I smiled up, to find myself looking into two blind eyes.

"Thank you for being a good sport." His tone implied I had done something wonderful. Somehow, Burton had hung on through it all. Caitlin looked ready to charge after the roughnecks. "Those no-good bums. . . ."

"That's enough, Caitlin," Gramps interrupted. "Could've but didn't. We don't spoil fun with could'ves. Let's end it there."

Grandfather required help crossing streets, true. However, as Official-Aide-de-Camp-for- Grandchildren -- or anyone else, for that matter-- he created an unassisted aura of angelic good cheer.

Ella

As she came out of Central Park, Ella slipped and fell smack on her back in the slushy snow. I ran to help as she struggled to get up. Her woolen hat had fallen from her head making her heavy skirt and dark skin form a chiaroscuro pattern against the snow. "Are you okay? Anything hurt?" I was certain she'd broken something. But once righted, cane firmly in hand, she grinned, a broad, honest-to-goodness, wide-awake grin. "I'm right as rain, honey." She brushed snow from her heavy coat. Gnarled fingers curled her gloves, but her laugh rang clearly.   I looked into eyes reflecting sunlight on snow.

"You sure nothing hurts? That was a bad fall."

"Nothing," she snapped, quick as a rubber band. "If it did, don't you think I have the sense to say so?   Just because I'm old doesn't mean I can't think straight!"

"Gotcha." Impulsively, I gave her a big hug.

"Come on." She pointed the cane "Walk me home. I'm not that far away."

I held her arm. She wound her fingers through mine as we maneuvered through slippery slushy Central Park West. At 85th she turned. "My street." She stepped carefully down two stone steps that led to a one-room, basement apartment.

"Welcome to Buckingham Palace." She bowed her head, haloed by bold, black braids. She opened the door. "Come in. Come in. Sit here." She led me to a spacious red-plush armchair with matching ottoman. She set a kettle

65

to boil on a two-burner hot plate, then faced me, reclining on a chaise with a bewitching grace Marlene Dietrich might have envied. "I've lived here ten years, bought it three years ago when the building went co-op. On a wintry day like this, it's almost as dark in here as I am, but I'm pleased to have this little corner of my own free and clear."

"Nothing beats having your own. I like it."

"How about a nice cup of hot tea?" Without waiting for my reply, she opened the glass door of a teak cabinet and took out two Belleek cups and saucers. She placed them on an oblong teak table. "I enjoy company, cooking. I don't entertain all that much anymore, though."

"I know what you mean. I've cut down, too. You've furnished your home handsomely."

"Believe it or not," her laugh rose from deep within her chest, "most of it comes right off the streets. I never stops being surprised at what New Yorkers throw away."

"You scavenge?" I'd found a kindred spirit. "I'm always snooping . . . found great stuff, too. Once I retrieved a Chinese red porcelain prancing horse from our apartment incinerator. A guy who works at the Metropolitan finds it irresistible and threatens to steal it for the Museum."

Ella and I remained in touch as long as I lived in the city but lost track when I moved to Vermont. A letter and Christmas Card were returned "Unknown. No forwarding address." One of her lighthearted escapades still makes me chuckle:

We had picnicked in Riverside Park. As we passed a basketball court on our way home, a ball bounced toward us. Before you could say "Michael Jordan," Ella scooped it, cradled it, threw it to a wire-thin kid under the basket who almost failed to catch it because of his astonishment at Ella's speed and accuracy . . . Whoops of approving comments came from the boys. "You with the Bulls," the

67

kid asked. "Where'dja learn to handle a ball like that?" He tossed it back to Ella. She dribbled onto the court, shot a basket. With a nonchalant hand wave and head toss, she warned them "not to catch me next time until after I've had a few warm ups." With Jessye Norman majesty, she left them in gape-mouthed awe.

Dear Ella, wherever you and your laughing heart are, bless you!

Ruth Haller

From the *Providence Sunday Journal* of August 6.1998, comes a story by Felice J. Freyer that epitomizes those who take life lightly and decisively sink the image of OLD disappearing beneath waters of oblivion.

Angel extraordinaire, 82 years old Ruth Haller, completed her second 1.7 mile annual Save the Bay Swim from Newport to Jamestown, Rhode Island in about an hour and 45 minutes, or 119 laps in a 25-yard pool. The oldest swimmer of the 300 participants, despite a relentless wind whipping salt water into her eyes and mouth so that "you feel like you're not getting anywhere," Ruth conceded that she had to finish. "It would have been embarrassing to have drowned."

Ruth's first swim began because of a joke. "A retired schoolteacher from West Kingston," Freyer writes, "Haller had been swimming since age 60, working up to five miles a week." Impressed with her devotion, friends suggested she was in training for the Save the Bay Swim. "I'll do it when I'm 80," the athlete rashly asserted. Well, last year her 80th had arrived. "What could I do?" Having parted the waves with her boast, character and verve at the crest, in she dove for her first Save the Bay Swim!

That was '97. In '98, she could think of no reason for returning to pointless torture, yet signed up again with the caveat that rough waters would keep her ashore. Appearing on the Newport beach clad in a silver and blue rubber wet-suit, Ruth observed the white-foamed waves of

Narragansett Bay. Despite her earlier disclaimer and the roiling/romping sea, she plunged in. "I didn't realize it was that choppy, but once in, what was there to do? Necessity brought me to the other shore. I kept saying to myself 'you can do it.'"

Wouldn't it be fun to meet Ruth Haller?

Bestowing Angels of Merit Medals upon **Ruth Haller, The Plus Side, Grandfather** and **Ella** brings to mind a statement by E.P. Seligman, president of the American Psychological Association and a professor at the University of Pennsylvania. As quoted in *The New York Times* of 28 April, 1998, Dr. Seligman claims that "No one at any top university psychology department is engaged in studying the three central aspects of people's lives: love, work and *play.*" (italics mine.). He now concentrates his research on "positive psychology," stressing attention to the way joy alters lives for the better! Dr. Seligman and I inhabit similar realms. He doesn't know who I am or about my evening martini, but I bet he would approve!

Which calls to mind *The Measure of My Days,* a book no longer in print by writer, poet, playwright and women's suffragist, Florida Scott-Maxwell. Roddy O'Neil Cleary, associate minister of our church, put me onto the book now unfortunately out of print. "There is youth in me, in most of us, who would be carefree and happy. I hear without surprise someone in me saying: 'But life is delicious, what beauty, what interest. I wouldn't have missed it for the world. Look at the day, feel the air, you see for yourself, all is well.'"

Is not that the epitome of angelic lightness! It reminds me of food maven M.F.K. Fisher, writing in her <u>After Word</u> from *Sister Age:* "What is important is that our dispassionate acceptance of attrition be matched by a full use of everything that has ever happened . . .to free a person's mind from his body . . . to use the experience, both good and evil, so that physical annoyances are surmountable in an alert and even *mirthful* (italics mine) appreciation of life itself."

And then, to close the chapter with angelic impudence, a quote from a questionnaire Dr. Restak included in *Older & Wiser*, asking if the answer be true or false to the statement, "alcohol is harmful to the brain and should either not be consumed at all or severely limited." "Clearly," he remonstrates to my gloating satisfaction, "'false' applies. For, when taken in moderation and combined with a healthy, nutritious diet, alcohol may actually enhance cognitive functioning."

I pounced on "enhance, " seconded "moderation." You notice, the martini in my title has no plural. Two martinis at night and there would be no yoga in the morning. Taking oneself lightly means taking one's likker lightly, too!

I also pounced upon "healthy, nutritious diet," but not with such obsessive determination that it precluded an angelically lighthearted platter of barbecued spare ribs –in moderation! OLD should and can enjoy itself by seriously determining not to take itself all that seriously. Adopt the habit of showering Peter Pan's fairy dust upon your spirit at every possible tide or turn. Forget about "if I had only" or "had I known then what I know now!" Nothing can be more dangerous and futile. You **hadn't** only. You **didn't** know. At this late date who's counting? Wipe your hands of the entire self-destruct process. You can, you know. What must I do to convince you that OLD means liberty! Not, however, without willingness on your part to step right up and grab it!

That's where yoga helped me so much. Practicing regularly improved my self image, my self-respect. "Hey," I came to recognize, "I'm okay, warts and all." ·

CHAPTER FOUR: Practicing I.W.N.B.V.: I Will Not Be Victimized!

Let's start with a vocal exercise. Speak--out loud-- confidently, clearly emphasizing each bold face word: "**I** will not be victimized!" Again: "I **will** not be victimized!" Are we communicating? Shall we go for broke? "I will **not** be victimized!" "I will not **be** victimized!" "I will not be **victimized!**"

Are you into the rhythm, straightening your shoulders? The mouthing comes easily. The practicing, of course, involves sustained attention, accompanied by conviction. Please don't grow discouraged, for the achieving secures you unburdened deliverance.

I can write this stuff since my credentials blaze with authority. The role of victim was offered to me in early childhood and I accepted without awareness of its lurking dangers. More learned minds can offer corroboration, but I am convinced a majority of us play victim daily as we go about seeking pity, sympathy, reassurance. I believe genetic chance, the circumstances into which we are born, the subsequent environmental impact of family, teachers, religious leaders, mates, all serve to enhance our Victim Character. Though presumably not responsible for my early trauma, a voice deep inside continually suggests I both contributed to and prolonged the problem. By the time of my Hurok encounter, the role had become as integral to me as the blinking of my eyes. Despite my vigor and vitality, I agreed completely that I could not possibly enhance the image of such an illustrious international impresario. These alternating swings between confidence and despair had formed my maturing; high highs followed low lows as naturally as the ocean tides.

Riding one of my optimistic highs enabled me to explore other venues. An accurate speed- typist in vibrant health, I wasn't all that unattractive--for forty-four, at least!--and had a talent for putting words to paper. That skill had gained entry to Hurok, at least. I knew the non-profit workplaces set less store on specifically youthful beauty, so I wrote to the Metropolitan Opera. Its Artistic Administration took me on despite my "age-disadvantage." Though lowest on the glamorous pole, I was on it!. . .And on a roll!

Innocently assuming all New York awaited me, I secured an apartment within walking distance of the acclaimed cultural center that was to be my headquarters The job and apartment complete with balcony, and view of the Hudson River, buoyed me to a new crest of optimism. What could go wrong? Ho boi!

First though, allow a disclaimer: My classic *A Doll's House* existence emphasized gentility, humility, cheerfulness and obedience. Nothing of my former structured, protected life had prepared me for the competitive business world. Alone on my untutored own, I compounded foolish mistake upon egregious error upon outrageous blunder, the most stupid being my resignation from The Met four years later for a contretemps I cannot even remember. What self-esteem had been mine went grinding down the disposall.

New York, back then, looked unkindly upon women "of a certain age" venturing forth unattended at night. Invisible neon flashed warnings that an unaccompanied female obviously was offering a public invitation for private assignation. The reasonable act of patronizing a restaurant for evening dining--with or without reservations--

turned mannerly, unescorted females into distasteful, unsavory nuisances who should know better than to emerge so unbecomingly at night. Receiving frosty stares, we are invariably seated by a kitchen door to either wait interminably for service or be rushed out A.S.A.P. When opting for a Night at the Movies, a woman all too often finds she's bought herself a Night at the Feelies, as, with the dexterity of snake slithering neath rock, male hand slithers neath skirt.

Timidly, I stepped onto the shores of the burgeoning women's movement. Initially joining seminars and workshops, my friends and I withdrew in shock before the strident waves of young feminists. We could not relate to their assurance and retreated in relief into to our Proper-Lady Doll Houses, safely entrenched on solid land.

In his book, *Live Long, Die Fast,* (Fairview Press, 1997) Vermonter John H. Bland, M.D., writes "Self-esteem is a great asset, but how do you secure it? . . .self-esteem is something you have learned, and, like anything else learned, can be changed." Bland continues, "You gain self-esteem by restructuring your cognitive techniques . . . by the way you feel about yourself." i.e., de-victimizing. "This may be a seminal concept to internalize first . . . not everyone feels like a winner, but even if you're 104 years old --especially if you're 104 years old-- you're someone special and you can convince yourself of that." Can? Had the perceptive doctor written his book in 1962 instead of 1997, would his certainty of "can" remain?

Let's do a for instance:

My next job landed me in the secretarial pool of a multinational firm headquartered on The Avenue of the Americas (which all reasonable New Yorkers continue to call "Sixth Avenue.") On the second morning of my employment, came a voice over the intercom, "send a girl to take letters." (Back then, all secretaries were "girls," regardless of age, and the IBM Selectric ranked Top of the

Line for a modern business office. Fancy that!). "Your turn, Carol, to deal with this guy." Jill gave me a wiseacre look. "Be prepared to play his game."

"His game?"

"We call him 'breast beater.' He fondles our boobs be they big, small, or like me, practically nonexistent, each time we're in his office."

"You let him?"

". . .Hey, what planet do you come from? Jobs that pay like this with the benefits and little pressure . . . they're not easy to come by, ya know."

"But . . . but . . . "

". . .Cool it, kid! It goes with the job description. We take turns. Glad he's the only

one. You get used to it, and it is only boobs!"

"Only boobs" or not, when it came my turn, I pushed his hands away, surprised at my temerity. He, too, seemed surprised but failed to press the point, so to speak! (I'm not making this up, you know!) A minor set back for him, but a major step forward in non-victimization for me. As with the Hurok insult, such behavior now would result in costly legal settlements.

I.W.N.B.V. not only hadn't occurred to my intimidated psyche, if someone had recommended the tactic, I would think they were speaking in tongues. Yet my courage and self-image began to improve slowly. After securing a position as a member of the Department of Development and Public Affairs of the American Museum of Natural History, the theory began to take precise shape, especially after observing many women in the Museum holding leadership positions.

During office meetings, when male curators or board members criticized them, they stood firm, arguing effectively for their view or program. They did not hesitate to mock or put down male peers, not in anger so much as in bemused superiority. Wow! That's what I felt; plain wow!

Too, I came in for a share of compliments and applause. I found myself beginning to like myself. Another wow! I looked around at the women achievers. Their one common denominator consisted of self-approval. I knew the background of some through friendships I had formed during my eight years at the Museum. I never dared ask how they had attained their enviable assurance; just made up my mind to attain some of it, at least, by realistic self-discipline.

Which returns to Bland's "can." Here am I, vidence that can can! Along with much of North America and Western Europe, I gradually began to understand and accept the Feminist Movement. I became grateful for The Civil Rights Act of 1964.

More significantly, however, I came to realize that the mellowed OLD who lived through those bewildering, topsy-turvy years should be given and should give themselves extra credit for their endurance. A tome could be written on the courage, indomitable good will, and perseverance of the last generation's emerging ability to try coping with the perplexing advancements of the late twentieth century. They came so fast one upon the other, and continue to appear with mystifying consistency. It is impossible for most OLD to catch up, much less catch on. E-mail, w.w.w. dot coms, the internet! These complex concoctions defy mastery, frustrate so completely we begin to doubt our intelligence and lead us into self-deprecating depressions. Yet we hang on. We keep trying as we take hope from songs like Holly Near's <u>Old Time Woman</u> with lyrics and music by Jeffrey Langley in the 1983 album, *A Live Album.* "She said 'if I had not suffered, you wouldn't be wearing those jeans. Being an old time woman, ain't as bad as it seems.'"

Think about that!

When I was a child in rural Maine, indoor plumbing did not exist for most residents, nor did telephones. Radio was just coming into being. Wind-up Victrolas the latest thing! Housewives managed with iceboxes and scrubbing boards and coal or wood cooking stoves with, in bad weather, laundry hung nearby. Who knew from washers or dryers!

Returning again to Florida Scott-Maxwell's incalculably valuable memoir, *The Measure of My Days*, written in 1968 when she was in her eighties, she expressed the intimidating technological gap separating generations: "Being old I am out of step, troubled by my lack of concord, unable to like or understand much that I see. Feeling at variance with the times must be the essence of age, and it is confusing, wounding. I feel exposed, bereft of a right matrix, with the present crime, violence, nihilism heavy on my heart. Troubled by their lack of concord in today's society, the old deserve reverent respect for feeling at variance."

The easy-going, horse and buggy world they were born into in the early 1900s bears little relationship to the fast-paced, email world of today. OLD has nothing to hang on to. There's no such thing as a plain and simple dial telephone anymore. Their gadgets have become insurmountable.

Melinda Hurst, a member of the Board of Ethics for Cedars Sinai Hospital in Los Angeles, summed this up dramatically during a conference in Abiquiu, New Mexico, on ways to deal with death and old age. Hurst said, "I'm afraid of being left behind. Afraid of the fact that I can't figure out the damn computer. I think the gap is painful between people who are plugged into technology and those of us who aren't. Things went slowly when we were growing up. . .now you get a computer and six months later they tell you you need a new one."

The quote is from an article about the conference by Sara Rimer in *The New York Times* of September30, 1999. Jubilados, a Buddhist-based group planning to establish a spiritual retirement community in Sante Fe, sponsored the conference. Its objective is to point up the importance of sanctioning elders, of affirming their rights. It hopes to give power and courage to the OLD.

Once on a Vermont Public Radio program, the reporter quoted Ralph Nader as maintaining that "powerlessness is the most prevalent danger to society." Without power we become victims. OLD **can** decide its power place in society by making its own **O**bvious **L**ife **D**ecisions.

But **how**, I am frequently asked, do we get started? Empowering ourselves is not easy when we are filled with fears, shyness and know not now to be as outgoing as are you.

A definitive answer has yet to be found. I certainly have none. I can merely continue to point out what a mess I used to be. Dogged determination to change seems all there is to it. I don't want to appear flippant or casual about this internal, eternal struggle. I can only keep reassuring you that working at it is worth it! Refusing to be victims secured the Feminist Movement, strengthened Lesbian/Gay legitimacy, and achieved South African liberation. OLD must not relinquish power. It must secure its autonomy. We cannot change others, only ourselves. By such change within, however, we end up causing a dramatic effect upon the behavior of others.

Louise

As guests of their generous but critical mother, she, Louise and her two sisters had amiably assembled at the Boston airport to fly for a deluxe, two week, Italian Holiday. It had been years since they had gathered thus without husbands or children. By take off, excitement had time-warped the foursome back into wiggling, giggling school girls. The first class flight did nothing to dampen spirits. Nor did the limousine ride to the five star hotel where –still giggling and wiggling- they began to unpack, showing off selected ensembles. Louise held up a dress.

"You don't intend to wear that meager thing in my presence, do you," Mother's loud command putting an abrupt stop to the approving exclamations from the sisters. "It's disgusting, child. Put it back in the suitcase."

Without a demur, Louise did as she was told, reverting to behavior patterns from her schoolgirl past. So, too, did Mother's run-on directives and criticisms. With uneasy acquiescence, all three daughters mechanically reverted to childhood roles.

"Let's quiet down, girls, shall we? Your Show and Tell tactics are giving me a headache. I'll go to my room and lie down." At the door, she turned to daughter Ellie. "That necklace resembles something from the Five and Ten. Won't do, won't do, at all!" She began closing the door, then paused: "Oh! One of you put in a call for breakfast at 10:30, will you? That's quite early enough for rising."

"But that's so late. Half the day will . . .

"May I remind you girls whose money is paying for this trip?" On which comment the door slammed shut ending all further discussion.

Ending as well all joy of reunion, of Italy, and of admiring one another's respective wardrobes. Instead, they were furtively stuffed into closet and bureau as quickly as possible. None took time to appreciate the exquisitely appointed suite overlooking the alluring Mediterranean Sea immediately outside their windows.

After a week of Mother's directive, and her sometimes vicious criticism, Louise's seams unraveled. She long-distanced back to a Vermont confidante.

"Have you, perhaps, brought some of this upon yourself?," the confidante commented. "What if you took a stand? Spoke truth to her? Stood up for yourself. May I remind you, pal, you are now an adult, fully responsible for yourself."

Louise hung up, but not on the advice.

When the group assembled that evening, Mother stared at the short-short dress. "I thought I made myself clear upon our arrival, Louise, that outfit will not do. You cannot expect me to be seen in public with you. Please return to your room and put on something more suitable."

"Mother! Stop this, Mother. Now! Right Now! Stop. Stop this persistent, hostile faultfinding. This attempt to control my life. I mean it. I'm fed up. Stop or I'm on the first plane tomorrow." The conviction and force of Louise's words, so unexpected, so uncharacteristic, brought on an equally unexpected, uncharacteristic retreat from Mother. Before Louise's I.W.N.B.V. onslaught, Mother did a complete turn-about. The sisters' surprise and delight left them with no desire to analyze the cause. The simply and quietly expanded before her now almost gentle demeanor. The "volte face," allowed the quartet to spend their last week in Italian euphoria. Instead of remaining a victim,

Louise took a stand. By changing her attitude and behavior she effecting a dramatic change in Mother.

Wouldn't you label that an I.W.N.B.V. stratagem for the week?

Leon Stukelj

An apotheosis of I.W.N.B.V. appeared in an April 18, 1998 article by Kirk Johnson in the *New York Times* profiling a 99-year old Yugoslav lawyer and gymnast, Leon Stukelji (pronounced SHTUkel). Invited to speak to students at Dynamic Gymnastics in Westchester County, Mr. Stukelji, a six-time Olympic medal winner, stands 5'3" and weighs 108 pounds. During their interview in a Manhattan hotel, Johnson writes: "Mr. Stukelji positioned his hands on the arms of his chair, adjusted them to find his grip . . . and rose from his seat . . . extending his legs at 90 Degrees, held them there then flexed in and out, suspended. 'Now that I'm getting a little old, I have to be careful,' he said, returning to earth."

Stukelji advises everyone to "be involved, on the move, and do not give up until the end of your life." His barely undiminished vigor thrives "not despite his advanced age, but almost because of it," Johnson wrote, "through a life force Stukelji labels 'synchronization: combining the physical and mental disciplines of a gymnastics to a career in law that formed a fabric and way of life that shaped, sharpened and kept him young."

Continuing to quote Johnson, "When in his late 90s, he had become an ambassador for a message that can seem in an often graceless age of mega-deals, commercial endorsements, and petulant prima donna athletes as dated and faded as his Olympic photographs. An old world gentleman who bows from the waist and leaps to his feet at the approach of a lady whose hand he might kiss, recalled with horror 'the 1936 Olympics expropriated by Germany as an elaborately staged exercise in propaganda. Their red flag had the color of blood'."

The *Times* photograph reveals a smiling, happy man. With his wife Lidija, the couple have grand and great grandchildren. On their behalf, he is suing the former Communist government to retrieve a home in Maribor, bequeathed to Lidija 65 years ago as a wedding present from her father. "I'm getting older and older and it takes too long," he says of the lawsuit. "This is a scandal."

Several months ago, I read of Stukelji's death, and remembered that during his lifetime, the magnificent old, Gold Medalist practiced I.W.N.B.V. with a confident, comfortable affirmation of himself

Sally

For years, Sally and I made a lively duo cavorting across the Northeast Kingdom of Vermont and la Province de Quebec engaging in daring adventures despite Sally's enervating hip and leg problems. Frequently in pain, Sally refused to waste her time in self-seeking sympathy. Au contraire, bilingual Sally boasted bilingually that "cripples like me have lots of advantages." ("Les infirmes comme moi, on a beaucoup de privileges.") Should you decry the word "cripple," Sally would decry in indignant rebuttal: "Does my condition change if you say I'm 'physically challenged?' What rot! As a cripple I get to park right in front of La Place Des Arts in Montreal, rain or shine. The rest of you pay a fortune or walk miles." (Si je dis 'physiquement handicapee,' est-ce que ca change ma condition? En infirme, j'ai le droit de me stationner devant La Place Des Arts a Montreal, n'importe le temps. Vous autres, vous payez une fortune ou vous marchez plusieurs milles.")

When I presented Sally my "OLD IS MAGNIFICENT!" crusade, she chortled, "I'm for it! I'm OLD and proud. Calling me 'Senior Citizen' won't make me one bit younger just as calling me 'physically handicapped' fails to alter my crippled condition one wit! Drivel, pure drivel!'"

Sally died twelve years ago. The legacy she bequeathed children, grandchildren, and friends endures. "The task of old age is the achievement of integrity over despair," psychologist Erik Eriksen wrote in *Childhood and Society,* Norton, New York, 1964. That's Sally.

Josef

"People tell me I'm nuts, an old man like me working as a secretary, no less, like some silly old woman!" Josef tapped his accented words out as clearly as he typed, eyeing me defiantly. "**I** don't think so." I hoped the denial assured him he did not need to justify himself.

Josef worked as a valued temp at the Museum for four or more years with occasional, unexplained absences.

It isn't so much the money." He had dropped the challenging tone. "It helps, of course, but far more important, the job forces me to get out, be with people; it gives me good stories to tell my few remaining cronies." His eyebrows rose in pure mischief as he added that "of course I embellish them. You'd probably not even recognize some, but they lap it up, the very ones who call me nuts." We shared a laugh.

Several weeks after the Christmas-New Year Holidays, a thick snow storm brought silence and emptiness to the streets of New York City. Came mid-morning, a third of the staff had yet to arrive. Not Josef!

"Whatever made you come on a day like this?" It occurred to me, maybe the guy's a little nuts, after all. Who goes out in such weather when they don't need to? Especially an old man like Josef!

He read my mind as if he'd seen the words on one of the articles waiting to be transcribed. "You think I'm nuts, don't you, for coming out today?" He looked me straight in the eye. "Surely you know what fun New York is in such weather. The City changes, grows quiet, friendlier, and really beautiful." A blush slowly suffused his bony cheeks.

"Anyway, I figured you'd be understaffed and need me more than usual."

We never learned Josef's age, but we appreciated his straightforward honesty and handsome wardrobe. One day we learned he had died. Cancer. The long disappearances had been for treatments he never discussed. We missed him, his wisdom and good sense. He refused to be victimized until the very end. I remember him as another star example of I.W.N.B.V

I remember, too, an experience last year on a Wednesday afternoon in the framing department of the Ben Franklin store in South Burlington. I asked about a senior discount since my purchases had come to more than $100. "We give them, but only on Tuesdays, ten percent."

"Well then, I'll come back next Tuesday, okay?"

"The store should give the discount every day to old people," the manager said, turning to the young man waiting on me. "Give her the discount anyway," she told him. "Why make her come back?" He shrugged in agreement. "I'm for it." She thumped the counter with the ruler in her hand. "Every last one of you has paid your dues even if all you did was help raise us. You've given service for a long time."

She exchanged smiles with the young clerk whose grin indicated which side he was on. "We should listen more to you and less to the big shots. If they were as smart as they think they are, they'd pay attention to your wisdom. It's awful, the way some of them treat the old!."

"I'm going to quote you in my book," I told her.

"Go ahead! I mean every word of it!"

She's right, of course. OLD should be listened to more. But we cannot change others, only ourselves. OLD must find the courage to stand firm, practice I.W.N.B.V. I found the courage through chanting a mantra, a repetitious telling myself, like The Little Engine That Could, that **I** could.

Donald

He once told me of his two most deadly fears: flying and public speaking. As founder of a small enterprise that has grown into a major, nation-wide corporation, its demands made overcoming both phobias an essential to its continuing prosperity. Determined not to let them victimize him, he overcame them through pure grit. The transformation, I know, forced him to walk through fire, but, he explained in his typically uncompromising fashion, "It was something I had to do, so I did it."

No beating about the I.W.N.B.V. bush for Donald.

He died two years ago. His roguish ripostes, plausible philosophy and felicitous imagination will never find an equal. We miss you, friend!

Playwright Tony Kushner in his June, 1998 Commencement Address to the Communications Majors at Northwestern University, from which my eldest grandchild Rachel graduated Cum Laude, closed the brilliant oration with a 1956 poem of Bertholt Brecht that sounded of Louise, Leon, Sally, Josef, and Donald..

"I always thought:

The very simplest words must be enough.

If I say how things are;

Your heart must be torn to shreds.

That you'll go down if you don't stand up for yourself.

Surely you see that."

Louise, Leon, Sally, Josef, and Donald stood up for themselves. Though unaware of I.W.N.B.V. specifics, they practiced it with aplomb, achieving a gentle power and autonomy. They face their final years with determined asperity and spleen, serving as examples of another Bertolt Brecht stanza from *Everything Changes:*

"What has happened has happened. The water

You once poured into the wine cannot be

Drained off again, but

Everything changes. You can make

A fresh start with your final breath." .

His poetic elegance finds confirmation in Dr. Restak's book, *Older and Wiser,* previously quoted in Chapter Two. "It's never too late for muscle-building exercises," he encourages those willing to make a fresh start until their final breath. "Even frail elders in nursing homes were able to benefit from a muscle strengthening program which involves the brain as well."

The futile excuses of "if I had only, if I had known then" become the watered wine. Instead, take heart from the snippet bios you have just read, and the story of Late Bloomer Me. Work to establish faith in yourself, overcoming victimization as you gradually build a conviction of your own personal worth.

Only you can do it.

And you will! Just turn the page. . .

CHAPTER FIVE: GRAB THE FRINGE

BENEFITS

OLD gets away with speaking its mind, behaving impulsively, dressing for its comfort and taste. "Been there, done that" serves as familiar motto to OLD. Having paid its dues, OLD has nothing to lose. What can you do to us? Our success or failure has long since been completed. Since the U.S. of A. culturally regards OLD either as invisible or unimportant, our activities matter primarily to us. We have our setbacks like everyone, but generally,

OLD accepts other OLD with minimal criticism. OLD acknowledges OLD whatever it wears, however it behaves. Most significantly, OLD recognizes its personal responsibility. *Where we are exists because of where we were.* We accept this status quo knowing how unlikely indeed would be any significant alteration in our financial or social position. In exchange, OLD gains an exhilarating independence. Utilizing I.W.N.B.V. in accord with angelic lightness, OLD finds itself, well, yes, an inch or so above the ground in company with Dr. Seuss, in *Oh, The Places You Will Go!* (Random House, 1990) and the fun you can have! Fringe Benefits reopens the book on Bland's "can!" We can, indeed, make **O**bvious **L**ife **D**ecisions!

Age maintains a firm grip of emancipation despite physical constrictions. Our incapacities slow us down enough to permit spiritual introspection and to set our imaginations working overtime.

Visiting with octogenarian Bill in Durham, N.H. who had broken an ankle, we exchanged "good mornings." I added a solicitous, "and how do you and your ankle feel this day?"

"If I don't wake up without something hurting," his smile was pure rue over his half-glasses, "I begin to wonder if I'm still alive!"

Anyone over sixty nods in recognition. No matter how meticulously we care for our bodies, how stringently we follow exercise/diet programs, the implacable aches/pains of age become companions to our lives. We live with increasing hearing loss, dimming eyesight, walkers, wheel chairs, pills and even more pills; we live with them, incorporate them into each new day –albeit often consumed with justifiable impatience.

There's a flip side, though: when regarded with properly **detached** attention, these impediments place us in a State of Grace. They adorn us with a beauty **defined** by veined hands, fragile skins, and deepening lines. Rather than unsightly reminders of roads passed, they represent beauty marks from new roads traveled. When **we** proclaim our handsome antiquity, refusing to apologize for or hide from it, others fall in line. The OLD **are** beautiful.

At eighty-four, just prior to her death six months later, Sister Edmund in her guimpe and wimple moved with an erect elegance that called to mind the serenity of a swan. Deep lines bracketed the life-force shining from her eyes. Sister Edmund, once a student of Nadia Boulenger, directed music at St. Mary's Catholic School in Newport, Vermont for more than sixty-four years and taught piano to almost every young resident within miles. Since age six, my grandson now eighteen, had been one of her students. He loved Sister Edmund and revered her memory still, as do most inhabitants of The Northeast Kingdom (as that northernmost area of Vermont has been labeled) and adjacent Quebec.

We meet after a long separation. Her face lights up, convincing me that only my appearance could have pleased her quite this way. We chat of the many years passed. "Yes. Many. I'm not as strong as when we first met. I don't know how much longer God wants me to work, but until He calls, my joy in music sustains me and increases with age."

The words are echoed by Jean, an 87-year-old member of the Burlington Unitarian Universalist Society. Paralyzed in her left arm after a stroke that also affected her ability to walk, the accomplished pianist shifted her talent to use her good arm and continues to play for church, for troubled children, in senior centers, wherever and whenever asked. "I practice all the time. Without music, life has no meaning. With music, age has no meaning."

Jean mirrors the more famous, equally courageous black Canadian Oscar Peterson, for whom Concordia University's concert hall is named, "one of the most virtuosic of all jazz pianists, "wrote Stephen Holden from a June 29, 1999 *New York Times* critique of a performance in Manhattan. "After a stroke six years ago that partly immobilized his left hand, leaving him unable to conjure the rumbling musical earthquakes of old, he refused to give up. Instead, he perfected a sparer, more melodic style, concentrating on his right hand."

Oscar and Jean, firmly enforcing I.W.N.B.V. live with Honors in OLD because they are making their own **O**bvious **L**ife **D**ecisions. Liabilities become assets as they profit from the fringe benefits only experience and time make possible, enabling them to bring, again quoting Holden, more " reflective, tonal beauty rather than thunderous authority."

I had reason to enjoy a different, musical fringe benefit on the occasion of my eightieth birthday: Daughter Madeleine and her husband Stephen produced a State of the Art Celebration in their West Charleston, Vermont home.

It centered upon the debut of cabaret chanteuse, Selma Crevoshay, 82, Steve's mother and my great good friend. Before an audience of 40-odd and accompanied by the fifty-something concert pianist Pina Antonelli-Chapman, Selma blended elegance with seduction and charm, to present an emotionally endearing program of "songs selected in your honor, Carol." With the poise of a seasoned pro, the Octogenarian Debutante held her audience in thrall. A round, all-around woman with short-cropped, gray-white curls, Selma glowed as showstopping beautiful. A young Selma never could have delivered such a tour-de-force nor received such an ovation. Only the processing of time enabled the old woman to synchronize and encapsulate her experiences into meaningful, loving-kindness that generated the power of her performance.

Within the past three years, Selma lost her husband and oldest son. She had diabetes, foot problems, arthritis.

Withal, her spirit endured. You might as well go fight City Hall as try to keep this I.W.N.B.V. angelic, old lady down!

Selma left us on January 15--physically, that is. Her magnificent oldness has embedded itself within the psyche of all those fortunate enough to have come within her aura.

Make way for similar Selmas. They surface with increasing frequency. Visit *Wake Robin*, a senior residence in Shelburne, Vermont Discover the bold, innovative paintings and photographs fashioned by men and women in various stages of precarious health. Read their exquisitely limned poetry; attend one of their masterful musicales. All this became possible through a spontaneously established program several years ago whereby experienced professionals in Wake Robin teach their less accomplished neighbors. The fringe benefits take on mutual appreciation compatibility.

Such activities abound in the Agencies on Aging throughout the country as well as in modest retirement homes such as The Ruggles House in Burlington, where intellectually formidable games such as Triple Scrabble become regular evening competitive rituals. The give-and-take that accompanies such gatherings makes possible the emergence of an inherent creativity which has been around, untapped, all along. It takes time for the heady freedom of age to sink fully in. When it does, duck. This is a warning. Numberless OLD will take up the gauntlet and dare to take chances cavorting with their peers as they reveal all manner of previously unsuspected talents. Cup runneth over in the Fringe Benefits Department.

In Hillsdale, NY, Robert, 80, continues fashioning furniture to give to friends despite a major hip replacement whilst in Pinehurst, NC, another Robert, 82, golfs regularly while his wife keeps her sixty-something year-old eyes on the ball since he has been declared legally blind. Eighty-six-year-old brother Eugene, of Pointe Claire, Quebec, wins Senior Olympic Swimming medals even with a replaced aortic heart valve and despite a prostate operation four years ago.

As for my eighty-four-year-old, brother Godfrey in San Francisco, he never lets up of his crusade on the importance of our jury trial system. Recognized as a leading authority on the subject, he has written two authoritative books and has another in the works. He merits respect, for he somehow manages still to hold down a job while caring patiently for a wife lost to him through Alzheimers. Then we come upon gallant Adele in Southfield, Michigan, where, at 95, we find her working on a family history album despite two previous heart operations in as many years.

Were we to ask any of the above how they handled their pain, overcame the fear and depression that invariably encompass illness, each would offer a different answer. I venture, however, that life force and will to live serve as a meaningful basis. But I know that the tender, loving care, and The Beatles' "help from friends," that each received became paramount. Others rely "upon the kindness of strangers," according to Blanche Dubois in Tennessee Williams's *Streetcar Named Desire.* Such kindness enhances the lives of the care-givers who know that such attention lessens the depression and loneliness all too frequently facing the OLD.

Think about that.

In a book of reflections on aging, *Let Evening Come,* (Doubleday, 1998) Mary C. Morrison illustrates "the old-age paradox, 'loss is gain' for now we are free with a freedom we perhaps know not how to use, a new set of possible relationships based on interest and personal tastes, not blood ties . . . now is our chance to savor one of life's greatest pleasures, working with congenial friends." She points out T.S. Eliot's claim that "the old ought to be explorers."

One such, Maggie Kuhn, diminutive founder of "The Gray Panthers," maintained her energy and high spirits by "committing at least one outrageous act a day."

I try to act outrageously–not criminally--if not every day, at least once a week. I commend the exercise to your attention. A favorite involves a clown nose I often carry. On a whim, out it comes. One afternoon on an interminably long, slow line at the supermarket, I put it in place. Reactions varied, but the atmosphere brightened noticeably. In the club car of a snow-slowdown on the Amtrak from Essex Junction, Vermont to Stamford, Connecticut, I passed several noses around, converting train to plane so fast did time fly. A Mary Poppins chum whistles as she walks, occasionally she skips. Great idea, that, a brief skip, if the old bod can handle it! ***Fringe Benefits*** in bold italics! Quite possibly only the OLD can get away with such frivolous frivolity.

A memorable Outrageous Act under a bridge in New York City's Central Park came to me second hand: Seventy-year-old Lily pushed wheelchair-bound Peter toward an underpass from whence, with increasing force, issued singing of contagious appeal. Cautiously, they edged forward to peek. A man scarcely five feet tall stood, back arched, head tilted high. He never noticed their arrival. Lily began to edge away just as he spied them. His proud body shriveled into discarded driftwood, so rapid was his defeat.

"Please, don't stop. We were enjoying it. We both know that feeling, the need to let go." He backed off eyeing them warily. "No. See. We'll join you, isn't that okay?" Dazed, he watched with increasing alarm as they began howling raucously. "You're crazy . . . " He backed away further, his voice scarcely audible " . . . both of you're out of . . ."

His critique of their performance was interrupted as three preteens on bikes came to a screeching halt. "What the fuck?" The blue eyes of the girl flashed angrily. "What kinda shit's going on here!" She raised the front wheel upright, then slammed it on the cement. "What the fuck are you assholes doing. Ya some kinda queers, 'r something?" She straddled the bike, walking it ominously toward Peter, waving her fist

"Just who're ya callin' asshole, asshole!" Lily let go in a voice that sent shock waves through Peter. "We're fuck'n hollerin' 's what we're doin'! Wanna make something of it?" She raised her fist ready to charge when Peter, unable to help himself, defused the threatening posture with bursts of uncontrollable laughter. "Yeah, look at us two old farts howling our fuckin' heads off! Try it! You'll like it." He couldn't stop laughing. The driftwood man stopped edging out of the tunnel as Peter roared his challenge: "C'mawn. I **dare** ya!"

116

Six unlikely confederates began howling into the arched enclosure raising such an unbecoming yet genial cacophony that they lured bewildered curiosity seekers to serve as dumfounded audience.

Though they scanned them carefully the next day, nothing appeared in the papers to explain the ten minute Monty Python production that had set New York's Central Park on its blase ear. Shedding the panic that Lily confessed they both felt, they had launched an I.W.N.B.V. tactic, committing their outrageous act lightly. Bet my snapshot of me and Maria Callas against your Charlie Parker album they got away with it only because they are old. But then, only OLD dares try!

And OLD simply must will itself to **keep** trying. I return yet again to this point of **no** return: either you do or you don't. The "I can" mantra bears fruit only if seeded by you. Go for it. Go for the little help from one's friends or strangers. Remember, though, the help won't help if **you** fail to help it along! Inevitably, the buck stops directly in front of you, only you.

Which allows for a shift of gears onto OLD's Street of Extra-Cash-In-Pocket on the corner of Fringe Benefit Boulevard. As our numbers grow, (and they do!) we represent increasingly crucial dollar profits in the business world. Our good opinion of stores, movies, and products makes a solid impact. We must make them known as we persistently seek that extra bit of service or monetary dividend. Remember we have already paid our dues and earned those special attentions and discounts.

You'd better believe it! With seasoned irony, we accept them, understanding well that they are offered simply to insure our patronage, so desirable during those daytime hours when the CEO Big Spenders remain glued to their computer Windows's seats!

Retailers will use all possible lures to beguile us into the marketplace, accompanied by a wily sales pitch to separate us from our monthly Social Security checks. I say: "Come on OLD! We're onto their capital gains game, eating into our capital for their gain. We'll play it, but according to **our** rules, resisting any bullying attempts, standing firm in our demand for Fringe Benefits." After all, perks is perks! We not only want ours, we want them with full quality for our coins.

My mother impressed upon me that "You must always tell the truth, Carol. It's how you tell that makes the difference, all the difference." Ditto, it's **how** one seeks F.Bs. that makes all the difference, too. I often ask. I am often denied but I have planted an idea.

Local, Mom and Pop establishments gain by sensible attitudes toward elderly customers. Several months ago, I was presented with a $50 gift certificate for use in any Burlington Church Street emporium. I entered a dress shop. After the customary pleasantries, I mentioned the unexpected bounty, adding "and do you offer a senior discount?" Accompanied by the cool, cold "no" was a cooler, colder disdain.

"Lose one, gain one," thought I, remembering father's admonition that "you can only be insulted if you want to be," an ideal I.W.N.B.V. stratagem. Ergo, neither insulted nor victimized, I sauntered down the avenue to another classy clothier. Sienna-eyed Cindy, the manager, met my question with ebullient good will: "We give discounts. Step right this way!"

There ensued a shopping spree that exceeded the $50, of course, but sent me home handsomely outfitted for the entire spring and summer. And not altogether incidentally, produced an unanticipated afternoon's entertainment. Note Cool, Cold: her shop no longer receives my trade. Cindy, on the other hand, sees me frequently as well as referrals of all ages. So much for penny-silly-pound-stupid snubs to OLD.

But enough of that! Let's move to practical, cost-saving Fringe Benefits offered without the asking: parking and movie discounts; banking privileges such as free checking and checks, and in Canada, for instance, free city bus and metro tickets. We receive ten percent off almost regularly on our bus-plane-train tickets and car-rentals. More and more supermarkets and greengrocers give discounts on special days. Hotels and resorts continually engage in a discount service. Just Keep Asking. Repetition Elicits Results. Remember: You have earned every Fringe Benefit!

Lest we misunderstand, I take no issue with businesses catering to the **moneyed** old, to the men and women who live in secure comfort behind their walls of affluence. Boutiques on Park or Madison Avenues in New York and Rodeo Drive in Palm Springs rarely deal with those on a strict budget. However, should I be lured by a gorgeous window display, I promise I'll ask. In fact, I did once. The bemused, immaculately groomed saleswoman smiled:

checks to that affluent coterie? How many more dollars, then, would accrue to the struggling majority who budget meticulously between their desperately awaited checks and their life-necessities, all the while maintaining integrity. Among this latter group, no shame should ever accompany a request for extra attention, lowered prices, full utilization of benefits. Not ever, not never!

Nor will I allow the specious argument that by giving fringe benefits to OLD takes benefits from abused women and children, the homeless, troubled teens or those with a handicap. That's a nasty cop-out, a fatal, logistic flaw. A worn apples-oranges riposte. I enthusiastically approve their rights and privileges and work for them. These problems belong in separate files. The loneliness and frequent poverty surrounding too many OLD entitles them to each and every and all manner of benefits, fringe and beyond.

Go for it!

123

CHAPTER SIX: BE GOOD TO YOURSELF

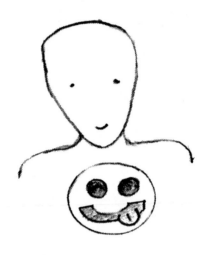

Go for it, indeed! Here comes your point-of-no-return: will you embrace OLD with inquisitive expectancy, acknowledge its nobility, confirm its entitlement or will you be vanquished by fear, inaction, isolation, and self-pity?

"The best way to face the complex reality of growing old" writes Sara Rimer, "is to talk (and I add write) about it." The quote comes from the *New York Times* article previously mentioned in Chapter Three on the "Jubilados Conference of Wisdom and Aging. "We celebrate the John Glenns, and the sexy grandmothers, but that's trying to transform old age into middle age,' said Rick Moody, former director of the Brookdale Center on Aging at Hunter College in New York, and author of *The Five Stages of the Soul*, (Doubleday Anchor Books, 1997). He suggested that "conscious aging is saying that the big adventure is the inner journey, and that does not have to stop when you can no longer ski downhill."

Exactly! That inner journey means practicing angelic I.W.N.B.V. and learning To Be Good To Yourself, as you optimistically prepare to make your own **O**bvious **L**ife **D**ecisions. My years of quixotic-exotic trial, error, and experimentation have culminated in establishing a more or less salutary routine that suits me.

Well and good, I hear the voices calling. Okay! Your OLD works for you, but how do **we** start?

Again, I find no definitive answer. Growing old is not, after all, a one size fits all set-up. Indeed, one size fits none. If these final life chapters are to be Golden Years, you must go for that gold using the suggestions presented herein merely as guidelines to bend and stretch in your own particular way. After that, you're on your own. I only ask that you acknowledge **your** life as important to you within the context to its relationship to those around you.

In the past chapters, I have explained my particular tortuous climb to my present primacy. I hated myself for years. I still go through periods of despair and self-denigration. No one has yet convinced me that my brain cells operate at full force. But I **have** persuaded myself of **my** singularity and the necessity for bringing **quality** into my life. Whatever years are left to me will be lived healthfully, vigorously and spiritually no matter my physical condition.

I cannot issue decrees to others. I can only ask that you get in the habit of facing your mirror determined to like what you see, to recognize your speciality and applaud it, and to establish your own daily mantra of self-approval. I made all manner of stumbling starts.

In New York during the middle 60's, I sat hours in painful lotus position at a Buddhist Temple. Later, as the 70's emerged, I studied at burgeoning schools with groups presenting amalgams of Hatha Yoga, T'ai Chi and modern dance; aerobics had yet to surface. I delved fleetingly into macrobiotics, flirted with Ayurveda, and certainly have read extensively. The result is a set of empirically based principles to which I am committed. Being good to yourself holds highest priority, with one major caveat: the directive in no way permits self-indulgent preoccupation.

Most of all, being good to yourself means accepting who and what you are. Despite the zillions who have gone before and zillions who will come after, none was or ever will be precisely like you --even identical twins differ! Think about that and respect your specialness. Replace negative self-criticism with positive awareness of your worth.

To quote from my well-worn *Emanuel's Book*, compiled by Pat Rodegast and Judith Stanton, (Bantam Books, 1985)

Humankind

is a truly wondrous manifestation.

Do not be so critical when you deviate

from what your imagination tells you

must be the perfect state

before you allow yourself

to claim the God within.

Do you see how limiting that can be?

Once the reality of your Divinity

is fully accepted,

you are free, you are free, you are free.

And when free, we feel good about ourselves, look more genially at others. What's the downside of that? In the process, remember our angel objective, to take ourselves and life lightly. I grow edgy and mistrustful of the ubiquitous tossing about of the word "love." It represents an entirely alternative schema. I can't love everyone. Can you? I can't even like everyone, and some people I really hate. But I try, I do try to remain compassionate, try to find the rationale behind their behavior, offensive as it may be to me.

It grows easier with age. Everything does. Our freedom remains beyond the grasp of those who are still in their buoyant youth. Perhaps that is nature's way of compensating. A Buddhist doctrine to which I subscribe in part states that "all suffering in the world arises out of wanting happiness for self. All happiness in the world arises out of wanting happiness for others." As with my hesitation about the word "love," I have difficulty with the word "happiness."

It certainly has nothing to do with wealth and power. My closest friend since ages three and four respectively, Phyllis and I shared an August 9 birthday. She married into what later became one of the Forbes Five Hundred richest families. Through our friendship, I became well acquainted with its members.

Tale-telling gossip plays no part in this book, but I cannot resist a mention of one party I attended many years ago. The living room was papered floor-to-ceiling with U.S. Treasury, newly minted, dollar bills, a concept the guests, to my horror, acclaimed 'brilliant and original!'" Hello? Anyone here for moderation? Despite their dollar flow, however, and their presumed easier lives, I noted their sturm und drang more than matched--in some cases outdistanced–the turmoil of those whose bank accounts might well have been labeled no-accounts!

Consider Charles de Clifford Roberts, Jr. whose money and power were devoted to the Augusta National Golf Course, where President Eisenhower often played. According to Curt Sampson's book, *The Masters, Golf, Money and Power* in Augusta, Georgia, (Villard Books, 1998) and reviewed by Lee Eisenberg in the April 12 issue of the *New York Times Book Review* of that year, the investment banker served as Sovereign Supreme over the grandiose club. He lived there in luxurious splendor during the Masters and winter golf season and then on Park Avenue in New York City.

"Not a bad life," Eisenberg opines in the review, "But was he happy? Having created the club, the tournament and the aura that went with them, he ended his own earthly round in 1977 by blowing his brains out on the bank of

Ike's pond, right there on the grounds," rejecting ignominious old age.

Happiness? Let's get real. Look into a report from Donna Murphy's Monday column in *The Burlington Free Press* of December 21, 1998 on old people: Connie Poulin, 105 years, "Whatever happened to my life, I went with it. Whatever I had to do, I did it. If things come hard, you can't say you won't do it. You do your best." Murphy went on to write that Poulin's life "has been characterized by service to others." Then she led us to "inspirational, 89 years old Judson Severy" who works with his son on the farm and regularly lends a hand to neighbors and friends. 'It's nice to help. It makes you feel good.'"

Money, though certainly of crucial importance for Connie and Judson, serves as comparatively small change in **ex**change for the quality of their lives. What I see is agreement once again with Mary C. Morrison in *Let*

Evening Come, mentioned in Chapter Five. "It is not what happens to us but what we make of it that counts."

I am reminded of my seven-year-old Madeleine when we visited her at camp. "Are you happy," her father asked? "Happy?" The diminutive imp wiggled her diminutive nose and cocked her head to look at her Dad's handsome face, so much a mirror of her own: "That's a silly question! When I'm busy doing what I like, of course I'm happy, not that I think about it, but after four days of solid rain? No, I'm not happy. I like camp, though, if that's what you're getting at."

Happiness just happens. We can't plan ahead or even work toward it. There is only so much happy any one person can be at any given time. Neither health, wealth nor weather enter into the premise. I thought of that this Christmas when my Vermont family arrived with Bengin, a seventeen-year-old German friend of Gideon's. Despite my sniffles and the dank, damp outdoors, the five of them, for fifteen minutes, filled my small apartment with magnificent a capella song. They gave, I received, together we shared a harmonious moment never to be equaled in precisely that fashion.

Instead of focusing on happiness at all, throw your lot to the miracle of your life in its poignant search for truth, beauty, joy. Quite possibly your search may bring you in conflict with others. Few of us see eye to eye. That does not preclude consideration of their viewpoints. Don't fall into the Lucy trap depicted in a *Peanuts* poster I saw in a Quebec massage clinic: sitting smug, confident, and arrogant as only Lucy can, the caption read: "Let's save time. Agree with me!"

Do, however, fall into the trap of giving humor its chance. Comes to my mind, a comment whose source I cannot pinpoint of Sir Max Beerbohm, that "of all the countless folk who have lived before our time on this planet not one is known to have died of laughter," or Poet

Marianne Moore's conviction that " not only does humor save a few steps, it also saves a few years." Moore lived vivaciously into her nineties!

Our liberation, independence, and success remain exclusively our own responsibility. After a certain point we cannot go on condemning parents, teachers or anonymous others who presumably ruined our childhoods. Being helpful a la Connie and Justin personifies a being-good-to-yourself ploy. They keep busy with necessary works and extracurricular good works without thinking twice, thereby moving easily into a contented, productive, gratifying old, old age.

Quoting from a "Letter to Mr. Horne of February 19, 1960, by Eleanor Roosevelt, and taken from *Songs of Experience:* "When you cease to make a contribution, you begin to die. I think it is a necessity to be doing something which you feel is helpful in order to grow old gracefully and contentedly."

Teens and baby boomers, take note: begin now to amalgamate such service into your lives. In and of itself, such care for others immediately gets rid of ego-centering.

The more healthful, upbeat routines established early on, the more magnificent will be your old age. OLD knows the emptiness in a life that is devoted to conspicuous consumption. Can young catch on early enough to stop its mindless rush to amass, acquire, attain? Insidiously nasty little organisms must be rushing around inside preparing these youths for heart attacks, cancer, and other early disasters. Certainly not being good to one's body-self.

But then, the body, per se, does **not** define you. Stop criticizing it, comparing it. Instantly, defiantly spurn forever the egregious platitude, "you can never be too thin or too rich!" Immediately, courageously sing Popeye's chant, "I yam what I yam!" Joyously accept the sensitivity and sensuality that your body represents, regardless of its size or shape.

The lengths to which misguided youth will go frightens the hell out of me. In an apparently serious article in the *New York Times* of April 21, 1999, Amanda Hesser writes of a group of eminently successful professional women who gather together for "skinny dinners." According to the article, these dieters "eat less, even if that means Diet Cokes and cigarettes for the first 10 hours of the day." As for the unsavory subject of sticking your finger down your throat, "Since when did that become diagnosed as illness," one telephone wire thin obsessive asked. Damn right that's an illness, kiddy! Bulemia, by name! A deadly serious illness, to boot. You'll all be lucky if you reach sixty. And can you imagine what bores they must be at a dinner table! Unfortunately, they are not a disgusting joke, but a pitiful example of how Fashion contorts people's sense of self.

I have a fat friend whose "price is far above rubies," but who cannot see how rare and wonderful she is. Embarrassed, she frequently refuses invitations; yet when

sauna. Selfish? Again, think! When you improve your well-being, you improve your relationship to others. The renewal radiates throughout your environment.

Touch? Touching is vital to every person's well being. Old people rarely receive tender touches. I hope someday to convince all salons to give low-cost massages and pedicures to old men and women; especially pedicures. Reaching one's toes, seeing one's toes, attending to one's toes often becomes a physical impossibility for OLD. Every six or eight weeks, would it be such a big deal for the beauty parlors to round up its elderly and indulge their tired feet? Think of the fun in the giving! The joy to the OLD in receiving.

That day may be long in coming. It does not mean we should not continue to ask. In the meantime, please! Do yourselves the favor and figure out how to beg, borrow, steal or budget such a monthly or bimonthly being good to yourself necessity. The return on your expenditures will be made up a hundred fold in the money not spent on doctors, medicines, confinement to bed or in persistent poor health.

As Gary Kowalski pointed out several weeks ago, quoting the Talmudic scholar, Hillel: "If I am not for myself, who am I? If I am only for myself, what am I?"

A slight inversion of the quote selected from *Songs of Experience, An Anthology of Literature on Growing Old*, edited by Margaret Fowler and Priscilla McCutcheon, (Ballantine Books, 1997) and found in Vita Sackville-West's story, *All Passion Spent:* "If one is not to please oneself in old age, when is one to please oneself?"

What better way, then, than by engaging in activities to that **you** enjoy? Say no to what you do not. "That's the way I live." a friend told me recently. "Now that I'm old, I can –barring emergencies, of course!" That smart woman has a proper grasp on OLD's unique freedom. Pay attention: Please! Please yourself!

In like fashion, pampering your body into fine fettle represents both a superb "please oneself" ploy and common sense, preventive medicine. It concomitantly creates dollar savings for you and society. The movie, *Patch Adams,* based upon the true story of Hunter D. Adams, M.D., though painfully exaggerated and far too rough on doctors, did prove how coddling and good cheer aids and abets ripe old age. Concentrating on your health --physical, mental, spiritual-- means not only being for oneself but for the community at large. Age takes on distinction when it works for others with "friendship, indignation, compassion," according to Simone de Beauvoir. In *Anatomy of an Illness,* (Norton Press, 1979) Norman Cousins explained how Marx Brothers movies among other comedies contributed toward his cure from cancer-- through humor came health. It's not that to me nothing is sacred. Rather, what is sacred takes on more poignant impact through laughter. It hurts sometimes, but it protects.

When Greg was barely two in our Maplewood, New Jersey. home, he and I stood smack in the middle of the upstairs hall off of which were four doors leading to three bedrooms and a bathroom. Greg's head was down, his hands folded behind his back as I lashed out at him in high decibelled anger for some small crime. He trembled before the foamed fury spitting from my mouth. At the tirade's height, Madeleine, not yet five, calmly walked from her room. Without a glance at me, she placed both arms on Greg's shoulders, turning him so that, profiles to me, she could look directly into his eyes. "Don't pay one bit of attention to her," she spoke with subdued command. "She'll be over it in a minute."

"Really?" Greg's frightened whisper had difficulty leaving his throat.

"Really." Hands still on his shoulders, she moved him back to face me. His damp, puzzled eyes searched mine for reaction as the wise, five-year-old's eyes widened in ameliorating alliance. I dissolved into laughter. We all did. How had the minx targeted my number so early in life?

"Against the assault of laughter," Mark Twin wrote in *Mysterious Stranger,* "there is no defense." (And as incidental aside: when it comes to laughter, does anyone have a more contagious one than Scott Simon's on PBS's Saturday morning *Weekend Edition*?)

Patch Adams, quoted in the *New York Times* of December 15, 1998 persistently believes "humor is an antidote for all ills," while poet, philosopher, essayist, orator Ralph Waldo Emerson, maintained that "it is the soul's highest duty to be of good cheer." Part of being of good cheer stems from being able to **accept** good cheer, in whatever form it surfaces, including generosity.

Last summer, Burlington was hit by a memorable heat wave. My apartment turned into a no-exit space heater. In two days I lost three pounds. "Mom," Greg called from Pennsylvania, with another example of his and Deborah's bigheartedness. "Take yourself to The Sheraton until it cools off. Send us the bill."

Savoring my lifesaving comfort, I told others of the gracious offer. The responses startled me. "What should a son do?" That from the bartender who claims he treats his mom right.

"Good for the kid. That's only what he should do." This from a stranded Bostonian whose plane was delayed.

"That's the least a child can do for a parent! In Grand Rapids, I'm building a house for my mother, and she has every right to expect it," offered a vibrant woman executive from Hawaii, who added emphatically, "I hope you don't feel you owe them something!"

"Maybe not, but can't I be grateful? Say 'thank you,' at least?"

"Grateful? Thank you? Yes. Guilty? No way!"

When I reported these comments, Greg readily agreed. "Of course don't feel guilty. We know you appreciate it, Mom. Not that a 'thank you' hurts, either!"

I don't feel guilt. I feel gratitude. I am lucky to have children and grandchildren who recognize OLD, respect and enjoy it. But is it luck? I have grown as wary of that word as with the words love and happiness, agreeing with Emerson that "shallow men believe in luck." Could it be that with our aging, we learn to accept the limits, achieve a found reciprocity? Being good to them establishes a master plan for being good to yourself!

In turn, spread about all that goodness and cheer to others. Take a turn at spontaneous acts of kindness such as carrying an extra grocery bag for an overburdened shopper, giving your seat to a disabled passenger, or just calling a neighbor you know is housebound.

One of the best originated with friend Judy in Salem, Massachusetts. She drives to work daily across a toll bridge. Once a week she pays the toll for the car behind. "Tell them it's an impetuous act of kindness," she explains to the teller then pulls away with a bemused backward glance in the rear-view mirror to discover reactions. They vary from suspicious stares, to friendly waves, even shouts and once to absolutely no reaction whatsoever! Imagine. I try it now and then. A day of traffic blues converts to one of the day's good news! Presto, the perfect be-good-to-yourself tactic!

It follows almost effortlessly that by being good to yourself you begin to pay closer attention to your health. You begin to block out time for quiet contemplation; for melding humor with sanguine objectivity; for judging yourself and others less severely.

The resulting objectivity begets composure, which soothes the psyche, sweetens the mind, and provides me with justification of the Kripalu Way, a model for being good to yourself training. The Sanskrit word yoga means unity, which Kripalu integrates through divergent disciplines, emphasizing the soundness of being good to yourself through the sacred trinity of body/mind/spirit, of which diet plays a significant part.

I am not a vegetarian. I care far too intensely about a fresh steamed lobster or a barbecued sparerib! Nor am I a teetotaler. I savor my martini. I am too much a hedonist to advocate a list of yeas or nays. I eat lots of fresh, leafy greens daily. Don't pin me down to my sources, but I remember an interview Vickie Gabereau held with an M.D. on the Canadian Broadcasting Company which impressed me enough to convince me to eat an apple a day (well, almost every day!), as well as a tablespoon of honey and three almonds. I drink buckets of water, especially hot with fresh ginger in it. The Harvard Medical Center claims we should each drink a minimum of a quart per day, preferably two! That's water, mind you. Not coffee or tea or soda or two cents plain. Water.

I spend two mornings a week working weights at The Body Garage under the guidance of supportive, knowledgeable trainer Alice Austin. The results have improved my muscle tone. I recommend it as an addendum to yoga practice, not an instead-of.

I favor chicken, organic, free-range. And here, I interrupt to quote Bill Geist in *The Big Five-Oh*!, Random House, 1997. "Nowadays it costs twenty-five bucks for free-range chicken dinners! When they stayed home, they were five and a quarter."

I find it impossible to refuse a thick, juicy steak from the grill and grab greedily at invitations to a lavish, luxurious, epicurean dine/wine on blanquette de veau a l'ancienne avec sauce veloute, particularly when climaxed with a creme renversee au caramel avec pure, thick, rich whipped cream.

I succumb to chefs such as Anthony Bourdain, writing in *The New Yorker* of April 19 1999, "Another much-maligned food these days is butter. In the world of chefs, *butter is everything.* (Italics his) Even non-French. . .We thicken many sauces with foie gras and pork blood, and proudly hurl around spoonfuls of duck fat and butter, and thick hunks of country bacon. I made a traditional pot-au-feu. Hardened veterans of the restaurant business came to watch the first order go out. The expressions on their faces were those of religious supplicants."

Sorry, vegans, I'm such a supplicant. I believe one can eat, drink and be merry about almost anything --within moderation, of course-- and still attain a healthful old age. The French Chef, Julia Child, now in her eighties, suggests planning ahead so that most of the week you eat with healthful restraint, then, comes a memorable night on the gourmet circuit when you can guiltlessly indulge in red meat and rich desserts

On the other hand, for specific, serious illnesses such as cancer, diabetes, heart disease and their like, I would not hesitate to give up my gormandizing. When health is on the line, no matter how rigidly the program, I would follow it. In my present state of good health, however, my buzz word remains moderation.

"Moderation," I hear daughter-in-law Deborah exclaim not altogether tactfully. Greg's eyebrows rise in impious disbelief. For they recall midnight raids upon their freezer where, come morning, alarming inroads have been made into Ben and Jerry's Homemade.

That's what you call exercising moderation of moderation, or quoting from Benjamin Disraeli's novel, *Vivian Grey,* "There is moderation even in excess." Are you catching onto the inconsistencies within my regimen? Its only constant remains my insistence upon compassionate, I.W.N.B.V. angelically lightened and blended with good to myself-ness.

A gauntlet often thrown my way, "with your genes, what's to worry," will not work. I do have great genes but according to Rowe and Kahn in *Successful Aging* that's no excuse. "Life style environment is more important than genes. . .with rare exceptions genes are not to blame."

Ergo, copouts become inadmissable, as cleverly postulated on the license plate of a favorite M.D. in Essex Junction, 'NOXQSZ.' (No excuses!) Dr.Robert Butler again. Remember him from Chapter One? "Attitude affects everything."

Within your hands OLD either assumes its mantel of magnificence or vaingloriously goes down in despair.

Two examples recently came to my attention. The first involved Anita, a diligently cared for wife and mother whose illness sent her into a bitter, continuous rage at merciless Fate, victimizing herself even in the midst of thoughtful nurturing. The second brought forth Ginny, ditto the above, who deals with increasing pain and incapacitation from Parkinson's with accepting cheerfulness. "When you wake in the morning, don't you sometimes want to curse your bad break?" Though paralysis skews her face, intelligence consistently lightens it with charm. "I wake up, open my eyes, look around my room and ask the air, 'What do you have in store for me today!'."

Little wonder Ginny's friendships are readily on hand to help whilst Anita's have vanished entirely. None appear willing to spell her husband's patient vigil.

Magnificent Old Age, even in sickness and death, depends upon attitude and fortitude. My attitude and fortitude brought about this book. Friends and students who adapted my program put the idea of writing it into my head. Others continually urge me to explain how at eighty-two I am–quoting myself from the Introduction--in my prime and yearly grow primer. Some few have asked why no one has yet tried to kill me for my Pollyanaism. My defense rests upon the despair that accompanied much of my life. I know about physical pain, sexual trauma, financial loss.

When Carol and Kripalu Yoga and Health Center in Lenox, Massachusetts initially encountered one another, bells rang. . .for me, you understand. . resulting in a consolidation of my past multiple experiments into one coherent encompassing life program.

My day generally begins with twenty to forty-five minutes of Kirpalu Hatha yoga and meditation. Pay attention to that "generally." Is it an indication of a weak character or flexible one? I've often spent one or two, even three guiltless un-yoga weeks. I make a habit of walking as often and far as possible. The practice enlivens my five senses and certainly improves the budget status of my sixth, cents, that is, as in dollars and . . . ! Walking ranks Numero Uno on any and every doctor's list and serves as the ideal for environmental conservation.   Walking improves my disposition better than zoloft.   As for

153

thinking, I do my best on a walk! Thoughts whiz into and out of my head in accompaniment to my gait which once became so vigorous a friend compared it to that of a storm trooper's, hardly a friendly metaphor!

Lost in the creative process, I have been known to expound paragraphs loudly into the disinterested air. Like today: Bundled against the wind, I set forth. Rustling the amber, wet leaves, I raised both hands high, calling to the trees above, "I've got it, my ending!"

The pronouncement sent a thick-tailed squirrel racing for cover. Four boys tossing a basketball stiffened. Unembarrassed, my arms swinging, I waved and watched their reactions as I sauntered away, savoring once more an enviable Old Fringe Benefit, getting away with all manner of bizarre behavior!

Would I, it occurred to me, feel so full of myself if it hadn't been for yoga, for Kripalu, for the steady emergence of my healthful regimen? I suddenly think of a quote from

Mary Oliver in *West Wind*, (Houghton Mifflin Co., 1997)

"Am I Not Among the Early Risers,"

"Here is an amazement----once I was twenty years old and in

every motion of my body there was a delicious ease,

and in every motion of the green earth there was

a hint of paradise,

and now I am sixty years old, and it is the same."

And now I am eighty-two years old and it is even better!

Let's examine this.

CHAPTER SEVEN: WHY YOGA. WHY MARTINI.

The Dalai Lama writes that "We must encourage our inner strength and work for a stable mind, holding to inner values of compassion and wisdom, qualities far more important than ordinary success or fame. If the outer enemies are destroyed while not restraining the inner enemy which is one's own hatred, then outer enemies will only increase, therefore, it is the practice of Bodhisattvas to conquer with the powerful army of love and compassion."

Such is yoga for me, a discipline that I believe holds a special, far too overlooked importance for OLD. Under certain circumstances, even small movements epitomize the body/mind/spirit discipline if they further the purpose of an exercise.

Example: for a year, I taught yoga at several venues, among which was a retirement home in East Craftsbury, Vermont. Most residents were incapacitated in one way or another. Sophia, a regal woman in a wheelchair, could not move arms or legs without assistance. She would watch, though, intently. I spent one session working with the group on the importance of focus and concentration. Sometimes, mere force of will helps to improve a posture, utilizing what I call the "Think System." cribbed from the Broadway musical, *The Music Man.*

The following week, even before opening the door, I sensed excitement. I came into a room of broadly smiling students. "Carol. Carol." Their delight brought sunshine to an otherwise dreary winter day. "Sophia has something to show you." Ninety-two-year-old Benjamin, labeled The Flirt by all, took my hand to lead me to her chair.

The slim, one-hundred-and-two year beauty tastefully jeweled and dressed as always, slowly, raised her left hand an inch above the arm of her chair. "Think System!" She spoke so quietly I could hardly hear, but she spoke confidently. "Look. Think System,'" she said again, raising her right hand.

I could not speak. Sophia had not moved independently for more than two years.

To me, that signifies ultimate yoga; complete, perfect. No guru master could achieve more nor would one hesitate to cede his or her place before the imposing elder.

OLD and yoga blend ideally. Through regular, nonthreatening practice, all of us heading for septo-octo-nono-cento-genarianism may look forward. I have seen first hand, as with Sophia, dramatic results. In research for this book, one example after another proclaimed the benefits of regular attention to our total well-being. The trinity of body/mind/spirit fostered in yoga enables students to attain self-respect, self-approval, and acceptance of whom or what they are. With gradual persistence, we discover the relative insignificance of those bodies we hang around with. What counts are our attitudes about them.

Christopher Ken Baxter, one of many outstanding practitioners and teachers at the Center, has written a book *Kripalu Hatha Yoga*, published by Kripalu, 1998, which I unqualifiedly recommend to any and everyone interested in improving their physical/spiritual life.

In his "Overview," Baxter writes: "In Kripalu Yoga, then, we are primarily concerned with freeing up the spirit. The forcing of our life into established forms and sequences is discarded. While we include very specific guidance about the physical aspects of yoga, and also provide a variety of sequences for students to use in developing their strength, flexibility, understanding, and stamina, our emphasis is not on accomplishing higher and higher levels of mastery of the form. Our aim is to awaken deeper levels of self-awareness. It is this middle path, balancing personal with traditional, internal with external, that gives Kripalu Yoga its freshness, vitality and unique signature."

In a recent Vermont Public Radio interview with Dr. Bland, author of *Live Long, Die Fast,* the book quoted earlier, this medicine man answered almost every question with one word: "Stretch!"

"My mother has Alzheimer." "Regular stretching has been known to help." My arthritis grows worse." "Stretching definitely helps arthritis." "I suffer from severe headaches." "Get into the habit of walking; even better, do stretches. "I can't sleep." You guessed it. "Work on stretches." For cancer, digestion, depression, even sex, "stretch" served as answer.

The decisive variance between stretching, per se, and yoga stretches (you'll excuse the pun?) across a humongous chasm, for integral to yoga, as opposed to most therapies, is joy, camaraderie and nonjudgmental, interactive support. Additionally, the discipline incorporates meditation and mastery of varied breathing techniques. The routine renews and invigorates: a perfect union for us ancients always on the look out for great, good fun within our physical grasps.

Misconceptions about yoga abound. Many believe it is difficult, weird, challenges religious creeds, even seeking to upset them. Additionally--alas!--many claiming to be yoga experts teach the practices as if they were aerobic classes.

Whoops. Let's slow down. I'm not putting down such classes. I have enthusiastically participated in them. What I am disturbed about concerns the difference between basic precepts in the disciplines. Properly taught yoga from my perspective, rests upon focusing at beginning and end, specific breathing exercises, and the establishment of positive self-acceptance by each student of his or her special beauty. *Emanuel's Book*, once more:

"True acceptance is saying 'It's all right,

it's all right, it's all right.'

Self-acceptance

By-passes the need for self-forgiveness."

Too many teachers neglect yoga's first principle, at least as emphasized at Kripalu: listen to your body. However you move--in conjunction with recommendations from the instructor–is the correct way! Moreover, comparisons and criticisms become solid no-nos'; only self-congratulatory pride of performance is permitted!

Because of a bedridden period in the 1950's, followed by a back operation for the removal of two discs, doctors meticulously, depressingly iter-and-re-iterated, "Carol, you cannot expect ever to walk properly again." My husband's agreement with their ominous prediction compounded its force. Despite them all, within myself I promised, "Carol. You **will** walk properly again!"

Slowly, despite discouraging lapses, I began to improve trying on a lavish variety of bizarre treatments none of which worked for long, some of which disheartened me dreadfully. Then seven years ago I came upon Kripalu and turned my life around. Remember, I've warned you from the beginning what a late bloomer, slow starter I was. Does the knowledge give you help and hope?

In 1994, I achieved my teaching certificate from Kripalu. During the subsequent years, I have watched spellbound as its teachers contorted themselves into all manner of cartoonist Saul Steinberg-entwined bodies. Not only will I never achieve such lissome elegance, I don't want or need to. Stressing again and yet again the crucial point: those stretches I can perform accomplish as much for my body/mind/spirit as do those for the rubber band Kripalu virtuosi.

Catching on? However you practice, when your focus holds, your concentration remains constant, the benefits accrue, one fast upon the others. Paradoxically, the more carefully and constantly you adhere to the rigid disciplines, greater by far are the subsequent freedoms.

Is not this so with any art form, any endeavor? Once mastery of the basic rules of the trade occurs, breaking away into all manner of imaginative alternatives becomes possible. Sweat not only precedes autonomy; but accompanies it. Remember Thomas A. Edison's words that genius is ten percent talent, ninety hard work? See? We all have yoga genius!

Some of you may feel resistant to yoga. I'll allow for that, with a strict proviso: Find yourself a program that suits you. Stay with it. Obviously, yoga works for me. I wish I had latched onto it sooner. I think of M.F.K. Fisher's words in *Sister Age:* "Parts of the aging process are scary, of course, but the more we know about them, the less they need be. That is why I wish we were more deliberately taught, in early years, to prepare for this condition."

Is this book doing that? I hope so, just as I hope readers realize I do not in any way believe my path is either the only or the best. I encourage and support those who participate in different activities. Swim, farm, play tennis, climb mountains, . . .the list has no end. But with its typing, a wee voice nudges: "Do they know that with yoga stretches, breathing, meditation, they will be even better served?"

Corroboration arrived even as I was working on this chapter. Quoting from Liz Neporent's article on Stretching Machines which appeared in *The New York Times* Science Section of July 13, 1999, she writes that the new demand for the machines "is due in part to the release of the American College of Sports Medicine's 1998 exercise guidance lines which, for the first time ever, recommended that people who exercise regularly should stretch at least twice a week to preserve flexibility."

In that same edition of *The Times*, Jane E. Brody writes of the importance of muscle building: "Whether you are a man, woman or child, by devoting just 20 minutes two or three times a week to strength training, the rewards will more than make up for the time and effort . . . strength training can prevent much of the muscle deterioration that otherwise inevitably occurs as people get older."

Both articles affirmed my yoga and weight resistance work outs. Brody emphasized that there was no need to "lift heavy weights that make you grunt and groan . . . strength training involves using small weights or working against resistance such that you are able to repeat the movement 10 to 15 times before your muscles get too tired to continue. "

If you find being good to yourself precludes yoga, I continue to support you --if and when and **only** if you stick to **your** selected "schtick" with committed heart and soul and sweat! Just that same old mantra repetition that "I can. I can." Intention is all!

In like manner, you may prefer an evening's libation of your own devising. I make my choice deliberately as angelic lightness spreads across the evening. You may prefer Black Label or be a Side Car freak. Even a Shirley Temple or Fresh Samantha proponent! Be my guest! Just make certain you take a load off at a hard day's end. Settle in a favorite chair, glass in hand, to contemplate the day's demise and the promise of tomorrow.

As I continue working on my personal growth–and working is the buzz word here–I'll let you in on a secret. A still, small voice of uncertainty persistently intervenes. "What right have I, Carol L. Winfield, to write this stuff? Sure. I've come far, made progress, become a successful senior reveling in OLD. Yet am I not still the phony pretender Carol L. Winfield, of the 1950s?

Then comes awareness of the reason why OLD and its concomitant, Experience, ring true. They can welcome a stronger voice that puts a stop to the inner-questioning: "You got here, didn't you? So just relax, acknowledge, and enjoy."

Easy? Of course it's not easy. Easy doesn't enhance life, only enfeebles s it. My dependable psychiatrist not long ago reassured me: "It is a known psychiatric fact that most of the accomplished, successful people in the world are consumed with inner feelings of inadequacy."

That happy comparison between me and the world's accomplished enables me to live more comfortably with my doubt devils and find myself increasingly able to retain the good in my life. I grow more grateful for its bounties that increase regularly. (Could this possibly be a result of my increasingly regular positive thinking?) I acknowledge the discomfiting past but see it now as making my present success possible. Harboring hate or vengeance places you on an accelerating merry-go-round of ever-increasing disorientation. Sacrificing them, on the other hand, sets you free. The OLD discover this simply by becoming old. Another Fringe Benefit usually overlooked.

So, too, is overlooked the way OLD finds its spiritual serenity and acceptance of death. OLD eases into it by the mere fact of longevity, of growing accustomed to both the joy and the sorrow. Friends and family die all around us and our hearts break and we mourn them forever. We turn to one another, nodding a so-be-it without need to express the pain. OLD appreciates the diversity of its individual members but understands well the common denominator of experience   drawing them together in comfortable acceptance and acknowledgment.   Well OLD knows "there's no center to life," as opera director (among other professions) Jonathan Miller said in an article in *The New York Times* of 28 November 1998. "It's all where you see it from."

Just so does OLD pragmatically accept its secondary role. As with attendance at a wedding, though the bride stars as cynosure, each guest regards the beautiful young thing exclusively from his or her point of view. OLD realizes that where once our daily presence loomed large, we are now no longer the cynosures in the lives of those around us and must accept our parts as guests. No matter, we cannot, nor should we, relinquish the intrinsic value of our OLD lives. "Where we see it from" now makes our impact more subtle. We play cameo roles, so to speak. An oxymoron has developed. With relief, we relinquish the responsibilities and priorities to our offspring actually welcoming the separateness yet bridle at their apparent disinterest in our lives. Don't the young scamps question where they'd be without us?

And yet! And yet! We have bountiful cause to cheer them on as they take our place. Just give them the chance. A memorable example occurred last week at North Country Union High School in Newport, Vermont. Led by Sherry Skurdall, dance instructor, Anne Hamilton, music instructor, and Glory Douglass, choir director, about three hundred students and adults joined together as a community to present a music and dance program of dazzling, exuberant brilliance. Playing to a standing room only audience, the participants pulled off a miracle. We couldn't have had more fun. Though exposed to decades of the "best of the best"in The Arts, one's thrill component can hit only so many decibels. I realized for that moment in Newport, just as with happiness, there's only so much enchantment and awe attainable from any one creative endeavor at any one given time.

One doesn't compare. One can't. Hearing Duke Ellington at the Rhode Island Newport Jazz Festival knocked socks off; but so, too, did the jazz band at the Newport, Vermont Jazz Concert! For very different reasons, of course, but each to do with excellence.

Excellence stems from disciplined focus on grungy ground work. Without preliminary attention to detail and a willingness to work one's guts out, good value never arises. The kids -oh God love 'em- of every possible size and background had done their homework well, bringing awe and enchantment in their wake, proving beyond doubt that when the door is shown, they will walk impressively in! OLD's job is to point to the doors, even open them. And, in opening them, let me close by emphasizing yet again– **if/when we are willing**–OLD's joyous freedom, opportunities to take chances, "go just a little further," rest there for the picking. It's up to us to stamp our feet and pound the table to make known the worthiness of OLD. By our attitudes and actions, ours alone, all following will discover that, indeed,

OLD _IS_ MAGNIFICENT!

EPILOGUE

(Eve Zipporah Winfield Crevoshay)

Carol Winfield is my only living grandparent. That she, of my four wonderful, vivacious grandparents, would be the one to live longest comes as no surprise. When Grandma Carol speaks of living fully and truthfully, by making **O**bvious **L**ife **D**ecisions, she ain't kidding!

This winter I had a great experience with Grandma. She spent the night with me before Grandmother Selma's funeral. The next morning we went to Dunkin' Donuts for a quick (though she took the time to force two donuts on me) breakfast where she slipped me $20, "Because I'm your only grandma now."

Selma's death was difficult for us both, but it gave Grandma Carol and me a solid connection. I visited her a few weeks later and had the best visit I've ever had. It was

174

comfortable and simple. She obviously took joy in our time together. I felt nurtured by her presence. We did yoga together. She took me to a movie and dinner. We made food together and had people over. But here's the interesting part: I'm assuming she wanted to show me off, but it's possible that she wanted to show herself off, as well! (Grandma Aside #1: Oh, sly Eve, you **do** have my number, don't you!)

It's always like that with her –she shows you off and herself off at the same time. These are her **O.L.D.**s, and often they fly in the face of what I expect of my grandma. I suppose that's just fine. By the time you're 82, you're allowed to be a little outrageous, in fact supposed to be!

At 21, I try to take risks, but often don't even know where to find them. A woman 60 years my senior has every right to seek out a risk and to revel in it. (Grandma Aside #2: You got the book's point, didn't you?) She has the right to proclaim things loud and clear, but it took getting used to. And, for a granddaughter to learn that, she must also learn to step back and give way.

As you no doubt saw from this book, Carol L. Winfield is dedicated to filling the space you give her –loudly! I give her credit for filling it in style as well, and that may be the crux of the matter. It may be embarrassing and difficult and counterintuitive to let your grandma take the spotlight, (Grandmother Aside #3: Oh Eve, I hope it wasn't too hard for you!) but after it's all said and done, how many people can say: "my grandmother works at The Body Shop, does yoga, and likes her liquor fine," in the same breath as "my grandma acts like the cutest little girl sometimes?"

If for no other reason than to demonstrate that she can do it, I applaud my grandmother for telling her story of triumph out loud; and, for no other reason than to show how incorrigible and sweet she is, I relished the opportunity to write the Epilogue.

I wish her the best of luck on her next decade or two -
she still has to make it to my wedding, dancing. I exp[e]
she will –charmed and charming as ever!

Printed in the United States
5961

9 781588 203458